Safe Sanctuaries

Reducing the Risk of Abuse in the Church for Children and Youth

by Joy T. Melton

DISCIPLESHIP RESOURCES

P.O. BOX 340003 • NASHVILLE, TN 37203-0003
www.discipleshipresources.org

Dedication

This edition of Safe Sanctuaries is dedicated, with gratitude, to Bishop Marshall L. "Jack" Meadors, Jr. Bishop Meadors has modeled throughout his ministry an unfailing devotion to including children in our community of faith and assuring them a place, a safe sanctuary, where each of them could grow in the ways that lead to life eternal. He continues even in his retirement, as an advocate on behalf of children, leading the Church to ever greater service and discipleship. I am truly grateful to work with him and to learn from him.

This edition of Safe Sanctuaries is also dedicated to my colleague and friend, Claire Irene Howard, Chief Executive Officer of the United Methodist Church Property and Casualty Trust, for her visionary leadership in preserving the integrity of the ministry of the Church and transforming our communities of faith into Safe Sanctuaries. Her work has helped the Church witness to the Gospel of Jesus Christ in many crises, and in every instance, she has demonstrated compassion, honesty, and grace. Although there may be many in our congregations who do not know her by name, there are very few who have not been blessed by her work.

Finally, this is dedicated to David and Kathryn Melton, in the hope that we will always be together on the journey of faith.

ISBN 13: 978-0-88177-543-3

Library of Congress Catalog Card No. 2008933047

DR543

Table of Contents

Checklist for Developing Safe Sanctuary Policy and Procedures

This checklist is a guide to assist congregations in completing appropriate tasks related to keeping safe children, youth, and the adults who work with them.

First Steps

- Read this book.
- Talk with appropriate leaders in the congregation, beginning with the pastor.
- Recruit appropriate people for the task force, as approved by the church council. (See pages 117 and 140.)

Task Group

- Read this book and discuss it as group, identifying specific issues for your congregation. (See page 117.)
- Begin educating the congregation. (See pages 27–43 and 57–71.)
- Set a timetable and make task lists. Allow time for congregational education and discussion and for thinking, discussing, planning, and testing. (See pages 117–118.)
- Develop a policy statement that includes the *what* (keeping children safe) and the *why* (theological statements). (See page 141.)
- Test the policy statement with the appropriate people.
- Develop implementation procedures that include suggestions from parents, teachers, staff, and others as appropriate. (See pages 43–54 and 73–96 and the list below.)
- Test the implementation procedures with the appropriate people.
- Provide regular progress updates to the appropriate groups.

Approval

- When ready, take to the church council the policy statement for approval and the implementation procedures for information only. (See page 122.)
- Plan a congregational celebration. (See pages 124 and 157–158.)

Consider these areas for inclusion in the implementation procedures:

- Nursery
- Sunday school
- Weekday childcare, children's groups, and other regular and special settings where children are present
- Youth, including transportation, overnights, mentoring/counseling
- Hiring staff and recruitment of volunteers (See pages 13–23 and 142–148.)
- Response to allegations of abuse (See pages 107–116 and 121–122.)
- Plan for caring after abuse (See pages 131–137.)
- Storing, accessing, and managing records and files
- Ongoing training of staff, volunteers, parents, church leadership, and new members/attendees (See pages 36–43, 45–54, 66–71, 73–96, 125–129, and your policy and procedures.)
- Regular review of policies, including the assignment of responsibility to a particular church office/committee
- Process for making procedural changes (and possible changes in the policy statement)

Part One: Our Mandate

Our Mandate

chapter one

AS CHRISTIANS, we are called to live according to the gospel of Jesus
Christ. Our Christian heritage derives from that of the Hebrews. We accept
the tradition and experience set forth in the Old Testament Scriptures as our
own. In the history of the ancient Hebrews, we find a deeply rooted legacy of
justice and mercy. (See Micah 6:8; Isaiah 1:17; Amos 5:24; Isaiah 56:1;
Deuteronomy 24:17; Leviticus 19:15.) We also find a strong tradition of hospitality and generosity. (See Isaiah 58:10-12 and Leviticus 19:10.)

Justice and hospitality were essential elements of the covenant between the
people and God. Worship was the lifeblood of the covenant. Throughout the
history of the Hebrew people, their practice of worshiping God in holy places
is recorded. At times, the holy place was no more than a small tent or a pile
of rocks made on the plains. At other times, the holy place was a beautifully
ornate temple with many grand chambers. No matter what the place of worship looked like, the people treasured it as a holy place, a sanctuary, where
they were able to worship in safety and harmony. (See Psalm 20:1-2 and
Psalm 27:4-5.) Today, we must remember that our churches are holy places of
sanctuary for the children of God. Our churches must continue to be places
where people of all ages can come together for worship, study, and service,
with the assurance that they are safe and secure in the community of faith.

The New Testament makes clear that as Christians we continue in a covenant
relationship with God and with the whole community of faith. The Gospel of
Luke provides us with two such stories. One of Jesus' infancy and one of
Jesus' adolescence. Luke 2:1-39 tells us of Jesus' birth and his dedication at
the Temple, eight days later. Reading this account today gives us a vibrant
picture of Mary and Joseph's commitment to faith and to raising their son in
the community of faith. Simeon and Anna are also included in this story,
providing us with the knowledge that the community of faith for Jesus' family was extended beyond their actual familial relationships to those who wor-
shipped with them in the congregation. Two thousand years later, in many,
many congregations, the same can be said. A new baby is brought before the
whole congregation, not just his or her parents, for baptism, and the congregation pledges, along with the parents, to raise the baby in the way that
leads to life eternal.

Notes:

_____

_____

_____

_____

_____

_____

_____

_____

_____

_____

_____

_____

_____

_____

But Jesus Called for Them
and said, "Let the little children come to me, and do not stop them; for it is to such as these that the kingdom of God belongs."

Luke 18:16

Luke 2: 41-52 provides us with a brief story of Jesus as an adolescent, as a twelve year old boy. In fact, Luke's Gospel is the only one that gives us any insight into this period of Jesus' life. Considering that Mary and Joseph began taking him to worship as an infant, perhaps it is no surprise that by the time he was twelve, going to the temple was the usual thing to do! Isn't that what we want every one of our families to have from our congregations? The opportunities to bring our children so often to hear God's word and grow in relationship with God and others that by the time our children are youth they will choose to be in church, with us or without us, because they have already learned that the people in church with them are trustworthy and compassionate. This is exactly what we aim to provide through all our ministries with children and youth!

We must live generous and just lives, following the great commandments set forth by Jesus Christ. Jesus plainly taught that children were to be included and provided for within the community of faith. (See Luke 18:15-17 and Matthew 18:5-6.) Throughout the history of the Christian church, children have been included in the worship and ministry of the community of faith. Today, the church may be the only place where some children find the unconditional love and care they so desperately need to grow, to thrive, and to become faithful people. As Christians, we must take our responsibilities to our children very seriously, always attending to their spiritual growth and nurturing. We fail in our responsibilities if we neglect to take adequate precautions against physical abuse in our churches. It is unlikely that we can completely prevent child abuse in every circumstance. Yet, it is possible for us to greatly reduce the risk by following a thorough and practical policy of prevention and ministry protection.

Child sexual abuse is a tragic reality in our communities. Although we would much prefer to deny the reality, child sexual abuse in churches is an inescapable fact. All too often we hear reports in the media about abuse perpetrated in a church or a church-sponsored program. When I began work in the ministry two decades ago, there was little public awareness of the existence of child sexual abuse in the church. Now, as an attorney and a United Methodist minister, I know that it is the single most traumatic issue I deal with in my work.

United Methodist churches have historically worked to assure that children in the communities were cared for with food, clothing, education, and an affirmation of value and self-worth. In many communities, The United Methodist Church (through its predecessor denominations) was the first to provide kindergarten for the children of the community, daycare centers for children of working parents, and Sunday schools where the children heard about God's love and presence in daily life. Today, these traditions continue and provide a solid foundation from which we can address the need for prevention of all forms of child abuse.

When allegations of child abuse in the church are made, whether they eventually are proven true or false, everyone in the church suffers. The child victim and his or her family suffer encompassing pain. The congregation suffers the trauma of knowing that its life-giving covenant has been broken. The family of the perpetrator suffers intense humiliation and a likely break-up of the family unit. Often when such allegations are made, litigation is the result. Criminal charges may be brought against the suspected perpetrator, or a civil lawsuit may be filed to recover monetary damages from the accused and from the local church. The costs of litigation, regardless of the outcome, are astronomical—financially, emotionally, and spiritually. These losses are experienced by all who are involved. In many such situations, it takes years to feel that the wholeness of the community of faith has been restored.

Even when allegations of child sexual abuse are proved false, the grief and trauma experienced within the church take an enormous toll. The person who is falsely accused and his or her family are terribly wronged and humiliated. The congregation is guilt-ridden about how abuse could happen in their midst; then the congregation suffers with the accused when the allegations are proved false. Finally, we must recognize that the victim who made false allegations is in need of the love and nurture of the faith community.

The 1996 General Conference of The United Methodist Church adopted a resolution aimed at reducing the risk of child sexual abuse in the church. The full text of this resolution is printed on the next two pages. As you read it you will notice that specific steps are to be taken by local churches, annual conferences, the General Board of Discipleship, and the General Board of Global Ministries. This book has been created to assist your conference or local church as you work through these steps. The 1996 resolution has been reaffirmed and continued by each successive General Conference.

Notes: _____

_____

_____

_____

_____

_____

_____

_____

_____

_____

_____

_____

Why Implement a Plan to Prevent Child Abuse?

Because our church is a community of faith—a safe haven and sanctuary—where children and youth can be confirmed and strengthened in the way that leads to life eternal.

Notes: _____

_____

_____

_____

_____

_____

_____

_____

_____

_____

_____

_____

The General Conference of
The United Methodist Church adopted this resolution aimed at reducing the risk of child sexual abuse in the church.

Child abuse prevention and ministry protection policies and procedures are essential for every congregation, not only for the protection and safety of our children (all those under the age of eighteen) but also for our volunteer and employed workers with children. We are keenly aware that local congregations differ in the ways they engage in ministry with children and youth. Therefore, each congregation's need for prevention policies and guidelines will be somewhat different from the others.

The gospel calls us to be engaged in ministry with children and youth. We must not allow the risks to undermine or stop our ministry. Rather, we must

- acknowledge the risks and develop a practical plan to reduce them.
- take steps to prevent harm to our children and our workers.
- continue to answer the gospel's imperative to be in ministry with children, making a difference in their lives.

This resource is offered as a source of guidance and of appropriate model policies for your congregation as it creates a substantive plan of child abuse prevention. *Safe Sanctuaries* can be a valuable resource for your congregation or annual conference as it undertakes to make the gospel's mandate real by providing a safe and secure place in which children may experience the abiding love of God and fellowship in the community of faith.

Reducing the Risk of Child Sexual Abuse in the Church

Jesus said, "Whoever welcomes [a] child . . . welcomes me" (Matthew 18:5). Children are our present and our future, our hope, our teachers, our inspiration. They are full participants in the life of the church and in the realm of God.

Jesus also said, "If any of you put a stumbling block before one of these little ones...it would be better for you if a great millstone were fastened around your neck and you were drowned in the depth of the sea" (Matthew 18:6). Our Christian faith calls us to offer both hospitality and protection to the little ones, the children. The Social Principles of The United Methodist Church state that "children must be protected from economic, physical, emotional and sexual exploitation and abuse" (¶ 162C).

Tragically, churches have not always been safe places for children. Child sexual abuse, exploitation, and ritual abuse* occur in churches, both large and small, urban and rural. The problem cuts across all economic, cultural, and racial lines. It is real, and it appears to be increasing. Most annual conferences can cite specific incidents of child sexual abuse and exploitation within churches. Virtually every congregation has among its members adult survivors of early sexual trauma.

Such incidents are devastating to all who are involved: the child, the family, the local church and its leaders. Increasingly, churches are torn apart by the legal, emotional, and monetary consequences of litigation following allegations of abuse.

God calls us to make our churches safe places, protecting children and other vulnerable persons from sexual and ritual abuse. God calls us to create communities of faith where children and adults grow safe and strong. In response to this churchwide challenge, the following steps should be taken to reduce the risk of child sexual abuse:

A. *Local churches should*

1. develop and implement an ongoing education plan for the congregation and its leaders on the reality of child abuse, risk factors leading to child abuse, and strategies for prevention;
2. adopt screening procedures (use of application forms, interviews, reference checks, background clearance, and so forth) for workers (paid and unpaid) directly or indirectly involved in the care of children and youth;
3. develop and implement safety procedures for church activities such as having two or more nonrelated adults present in classroom or activity; leaving doors open and installing half-doors or windows in doors or halls; providing hall monitors; instituting sign-in and sign-out procedures for children ages ten or younger; and so forth;
4. advise children and young persons of an agency or a person outside as well as within the local church whom they can contact for advice and help if they have suffered abuse;
5. carry liability insurance that includes sexual abuse coverage;
6. assist the development of awareness and self-protection skills for children and youth through special curriculum and activities; and
7. be familiar with annual conference and other church policies regarding clergy sexual misconduct.

---

*"Ritual abuse" refers to abusive acts committed as part of ceremonies or rites; ritual abusers are often related to cults, or pretend to be.

Notes:

_____

_____

_____

_____

_____

_____

_____

_____

_____

_____

_____

_____

_____

Why Implement a Plan to Prevent Child Abuse?

Because our church is a community of faith and a safe sanctuary where children and youth can learn and develop the spiritual resources they need to face suffering and evil.

Notes: _____

_____

_____

_____

_____

_____

_____

_____

_____

_____

_____

_____

_____

"WHY WERE YOU SEARCHING for me? Did you not know that I must be in my Father's house?"
Luke 2:49

B. Annual conferences should

1. develop safety and risk-reducing policies and procedures for conference-sponsored events such as camps, retreats, youth gatherings, childcare at conference events, mission trips, and so forth; and
2. develop guidelines and training processes for use by church leaders who carry responsibility for prevention of child abuse in local churches. Both sets of policies shall be developed by a task force appointed by the cabinet in cooperation with appropriate conference agencies. These policies shall be approved by the annual conference and assigned to a conference agency for implementation. It is suggested that the policies be circulated in conference publications and shared with lay professionals and clergy at district or conference seminars.

C. The General Board of Discipleship and the General Board of Global Ministries should cooperatively develop and/or identify and promote the following resources:

1. sample policies, procedures, forms, and so forth for reducing the risk of sexual abuse and exploitation of children and youth in local churches, both in relation to their own sponsored programs and to any outreach ministries or other programs for children or youth that use church space;
2. child abuse prevention curriculum for use in local churches;
3. training opportunities and other educational resources on child sexual abuse and exploitation and on ritual abuse; and
4. resources on healing for those who have experienced childhood sexual trauma.

See Social Principles (2004 *Book of Discipline*, ¶ 162C), "Putting Children and Their Families First" (1996 *Book of Resolutions*, p. 114), "Sexual Ethics Within Ministerial Relationships" (2000 *Book of Resolutions*, p. 135).

From *The Book of Resolutions of The United Methodist Church—2000*, pp. 180–182. Copyright © 2004 by The United Methodist Publishing House. Used by permission.

chapter two

Recruiting, Screening, and Hiring Workers

WHEN A CONGREGATION decides to develop and implement a comprehensive strategy for the prevention of child abuse, the best place to begin is with the development of appropriate procedures for recruiting, screening, and hiring the people who will work with children and youth. In spite of other adopted safety procedures, if a church does not include a thorough screening process, it will not provide the control and security necessary to assure the safety of children participating in its ministries. Each congregation should approach the recruitment/screening/hiring process in two stages. First, there needs to be a procedure for the employees and volunteers who will work with children and youth on a regular and frequent basis. Second, there needs to be a procedure for workers who will only be involved with children on an occasional basis. By implementing such a system, even workers who are called at the last minute to replace a regular worker can be recruited from a group that has been adequately screened in advance.

If an incident of child abuse occurs or is reported, having implemented a thorough screening process for the church's workers with children and youth and having applied that process to all workers (paid and volunteer) will go a long way toward demonstrating that the church has taken reasonable actions to protect its children. When the use of a thorough screening process is coupled with the regular use of additional safety procedures, such as the "Two-Adult Rule"(discussed later in this resource), the reasonableness of the church's actions is further demonstrated. In addition, use of a thorough recruitment and screening process may reduce the risk of false allegations being made against your workers. By making it known to the whole congregation that all workers with children have been carefully selected, indeed "hand picked," for their positions, you are assuring that only workers who will put the children's best interests first have been selected. Thus, people who might consider making false allegations against any of the workers will have the worker's reputation and selection as additional obstacles to overcome in making the allegations credible. For example, let me share this story. In a church that was a Safe Sanctuaries congregation, a friend of mine was a Sunday School teacher in

Notes: _____

_____

_____

_____

_____

_____

_____

_____

_____

_____

_____

_____

_____

If Any Stranger or New

member can have immediate access to our children, we have failed to provide the safe sanctuary we promised our children at their baptism.

the first grade class. Ruth, and her co-teacher Jane, welcomed a new group of children on the first Sunday of the new year. All of the children seemed happy and enthusiastic each Sunday. The teachers arrived early each week to set up the classroom for the activities. The classroom door was a Dutch-door and the teachers left the top half open so that they could see out and anyone in the hallway could see into the classroom.

One Sunday, Ruth was in the class room at the crafts table. Jane was seated in the story circle with a few children. Johnny, one of the boys in the class, came rushing through the door into the room and headed toward the story circle. Jane stood up to greet him, stretching out her arms to give him a hug. Just as he came close enough for her to hug him, he began to shout, "Stop, stop! You're hurting me." Ruth looked over toward the story circle to see what was wrong. She was completely astounded to see Johnny's father standing at the Dutch-door, videotaping his son's performance. In other words, Johnny's father had planned and rehearsed with his son a scene in which Johnny would pretend that the teachers were hurting him. Then, with a tape of the so-called injury, Johnny's dad planned to demand that the church pay a large sum of money in exchange for him not pursuing a lawsuit against the church.

Ruth stepped to the door, took Johnny's father by the arm, and escorted him to the pastor's office. The Sunday School superintendent, who was a roving volunteer, stepped into the class room to take Ruth's place. When Ruth got to the pastor, she explained what had happened. The pastor asked Johnny's father for an explanation. He said, "Your teachers have been hurting my son and now I have proof on this tape." Fortunately, for Ruth, Jane, and the pastor, the screening process used to select Sunday School teachers had been thorough and the pastor felt confident in Ruth's and Jane's leadership. The pastor was able to stand firm in his response to the man. He said, "I know these teachers and I have complete trust in them. If you have set up this scenario so that you could demand money from our church, you must have a serious problem. Won't you tell us what the problem is?" In the end, the man revealed that his family was in deep financial trouble because he had lost his job and their home was being foreclosed. He thought that the church would be willing to write a big check, or ask the insurance company to write a big check, to avoid bad publicity. To him, that seemed like a reasonable solution to his financial woes.

Instead of writing a big check, the pastor offered to help the man and his family in several other ways. The pastor was not frightened by the man's false allegations because he knew his teachers were trustworthy and well trained in Safe Sanctuaries operating principles. Thus, the pastor was able to respond in a way that addressed the man's problems without getting the church involved in litigation and without severing the man's relationship with the church. In the end, the pastor, Ruth, Jane, and Johnny's family were all glad that this was a Safe Sanctuary congregation!

Important Forms

The following items should be included in each congregation's recruitment/screening/hiring process for workers with children and youth:

- Position descriptions
- Position application forms
- Personal reference forms
- Consent to criminal background check forms
- Personal interview summary forms
- Personal reference interview form

Samples of each of these forms are provided in this resource (pp. 139–158). Please be aware that these are only samples, and you should modify each (in consultation with legal counsel) to meet the requirements of your church as well as the requirements of your state and local laws. The appropriate use of these forms will vary depending upon whether you are recruiting occasional workers or regular workers (both paid and volunteer).

Recruiting Regular Workers

For full-time, part-time, paid, volunteer, clergy, or lay use an application form that requests comprehensive information regarding the applicant's

- identification
- address
- employment history for the past five years
- volunteer work during the past five years
- experiences and skills specifically related to the position
- prior church membership (if any)
- personal references (not related to the applicant) with complete address and contact information

Notes:

_____

_____

_____

_____

_____

_____

_____

_____

_____

_____

_____

_____

BE FIRM AND STEADFAST IN your commitment to careful recruiting, screening, and hiring practices.

Notes: _____

_____

_____

_____

_____

_____

_____

_____

_____

_____

_____

_____

_____

THE CHURCH'S SCREENING procedures should be equally applied to all workers (paid, volunteer, clergy, lay) who will interact with children and youth.

- waiver of any right to confidentiality and of any right to pursue damages against the church caused by the references' responses.
- certification that the information provided is true and correct

If permitted in your local legal jurisdiction, also request that the applicant list **any** criminal convictions (even traffic violations since workers with children and youth often need to drive church vehicles).

Finally, include a space for the applicant's signature and date.

Reference Check Forms

Forms similar to the sample on page 148 provide the employer with an outline of the information needed from references, as well as a place to note the responses if the contact is being made by telephone. (These forms are also useful if the reference check is conducted through the mail.)

Interviews

A personal interview is not required for every applicant but should certainly be conducted for those the church are seriously considering after reviewing their applications and references. Use the interview to clarify any questions you may have about information on the application and to form a firsthand impression of the applicant. Training for conducting this type of screening interview is often available from agencies such as the YMCA or the Girl Scouts. If it is available in your location, take advantage of it.

Screening Workers

When your church begins to implement the recruiting and screening procedure, it will be necessary to have the appropriate forms completed by the workers who are already working. New applicants should be required to complete the entire procedure before being considered for a position.

Ideally, a recruiting and screening procedure like the one outlined here will be applied to any member of the church staff (paid or volunteer, clergy or lay) who will be involved in work with children and youth. Sometimes the clergy do not recognize the importance of following the procedures. Clergy have been heard to say things like, "Oh, you don't need to check me out. I'm a minister!" Or, "The annual conference board of ministry has already done all this and if the board says I'm good enough for this church, then I don't have to answer any more questions."

Responses like these put the church in an awkward position. The usual result is that the church applies the screening procedures only to non-clergy workers. We certainly hope that the church does not come to regret its choice. Nevertheless, it is necessary to remind churches that allegations of child sexual abuse are brought against clergy as well as laity. If an incident involving a clergyperson who refused to submit to the screening procedure is reported, how will the church respond when the victim's parents cry, "How could you let this so-called 'minister' be involved with our children when he had a criminal record?"

Even if the church is able to mollify the victim's parents, they may still face staggering consequences if litigation ensues. Beyond the financial consequences, the congregation will be confronted by haunting thoughts of "If only we had stood firm and made Rev. _____ fill out those forms." For the sake of the minister's integrity and the effectiveness of his or her leadership, it is far better to say, "Here is my consent. I want to set an example for our congregation and show the community that we are a Safe Sanctuary church."

When clergy persons do not cooperate in the screening procedures, they have little defense if false allegations are made against them. This not only puts the individual clergy person at risk; but it also puts the congregation at risk in the event of allegations or a lawsuit. Local churches expect that their ministers are of sterling character, and they usually are. Therefore, clergy should not be overly concerned about reference and criminal background checks. Once the responses are on file, the church can prove that it made reasonable efforts to screen staff members and that no reason was discovered that would preclude the person's involvement with children and youth.

In other words, full cooperation with the screening procedure by clergy staff creates a "win-win" situation for the church and the clergy. The church is able to maintain the integrity of its commitment to the prevention of child abuse, and the clergyperson sets a good example for all other staff. In addition, the clergyperson's good character is reinforced by the reports received from his or her references.

Notes:

_____

_____

_____

_____

_____

_____

_____

_____

_____

_____

_____

_____

SCREENING REDUCES THE RISK OF
- a child abuser being recruited to work with your children.
- your church being accused of negligent hiring practices.
- false allegations being brought against workers.

Notes: _____

_____

_____

_____

_____

_____

_____

_____

_____

_____

_____

_____

_____

THE SCREENING OF ALL

workers with children and youth, including clergy, creates a win-win situation for the church and the workers.

Recruiting Occasional Workers

The recruiting/screening procedures outlined for full-time or part-time workers are also ideal for use with workers who may only work a few hours or a few events each year. However, in a local church, it is frequently impossible to use such a procedure when a regular worker cannot come to work and the nursery is short-staffed. Frequently the nursery coordinator appeals to little Joey's mom saying, "We're short a worker today. Could you please stay in the nursery just for the morning worship service?" Usually, Joey's mom is happy to volunteer, and the nursery coordinator's problem is solved. Imagine the consequences if Joey's mom is later accused of abusing a child in the nursery during the time she was there as a volunteer worker. Whether the accusation turns out to be true or false, a crisis is created for the church, for the child and his or her family, and for the volunteer and her family.

How can the local church maintain its commitment to preventing child abuse, including a thorough screening of all workers with children and youth, and still have enough flexibility to recruit last-minute help? One possibility is to create a bank of potential occasional volunteers by introducing the church's policies and procedures to new members in their initial membership orientation.

The new member orientation could include

- a membership form requesting the following information: name, address, church membership during the past three to five years, volunteer work done in previous churches, and two references with addresses (if the new member is not transferring by letter from the previous church).
- An explanation that each new member will be asked to fill out the membership form before he or she is invited to volunteer as a worker with children or youth.
- An explanation of the Six Month Hospitality policy which invites all new members to take part in the ministries of the church for six months and then make a decision with the leaders of the church about where the member would like to get involved as a volunteer leader.
- A written copy of the church's policies and procedures for Safe Sanctuaries operations
- A covenant for the member to sign stating that in the

event the member is recruited to work with children or youth, he or she agrees to follow the church's policies and procedures for the prevention of child abuse.

By providing these things to each new member, you are giving him or her the opportunity to inform the church of his or her desire to work with children or youth. You are also giving the new member the opportunity to learn the church's policies and to either cooperate with them or decide not to volunteer with children and youth.

This type of new member orientation and screening serves two very important purposes. It helps the congregation identify new members who are willing to volunteer with children and youth, and it very possibly will discourage a potential abuser from any effort to abuse in this congregation. Thus, you have created another "win-win" situation for the children and for the congregation.

Staffing for Camping Ministries

Camping ministries are vital ministries for all ages—children, youth, and adults. Many congregations, and denominations, are engaged in camping ministries in a variety of settings. Careful screening and selection in the process of recruiting the staff members is just as important for camping ministries as it is in any other ministry. However, there are some special aspects of staffing that need to be considered in our planning.

Many, if not most, summer camps are staffed in part with youth and college age students. This creates the necessity for reliance on primary screening methods, other than criminal background checks, such as checking several references and conducting personal interviews with each applicant. Criminal background checks can be used; but, it must be noted that juvenile criminal records are generally sealed and therefore would not be revealed in such a background check.

A thorough screening plan for staffing your camp will include the following:

- Contacting at least two, and three if possible, references for each applicant to find out what skills and experience the applicant has that would be valuable in the camping ministry;

Notes:

_____

_____

_____

_____

_____

_____

_____

_____

_____

_____

_____

_____

_____

Notes:
_____
_____
_____
_____
_____
_____
_____
_____
_____
_____
_____
_____

- Conducting a personal interview with each applicant to discover the type of experiences he or she has, and talents, that would contribute to the camping ministry;
- Receiving a written application form from each person seeking a position that provides complete personal contact information and birth date verification; and
- Conducting a criminal background check on each adult applicant.

All of the information collected for each applicant will need to be maintained in confidential files.

The fact that summer camps are often staffed with a large number of youth and college age students calls for careful planning in staff assignments. Specifically, if the camp program or weekly session is designed for junior high or senior high campers, it may not be realistic to be able to maintain the rule of staffers being five years older than campers. If that is the situation, then it is recommended by the American Camping Association that the staffers be at least sixteen years old and at least two years older than the campers (see American Camp Association accreditation standards as www.acacamps.org). It is also recommended that in these situations, a prudent approach would be to arrange for an additional staffer to be available, on a floating basis, to provide an increased measure of supervision and leadership.

The primary purpose of the "Five Years Older" policy is to assure that we don't put children "in charge" of children. In junior and senior high camps there is another factor that should be considered. Staff members who are close to the same age as the campers may be more likely to have difficulty maintaining appropriate social boundaries. Experienced camp directors know how easy it is for a junior high camper and a senior high aged staffer to think it would be not only fun, but appropriate, to start up a dating relationship. We could often describe senior high campers and college aged staffers in the same way. Thus, if it is unrealistic to staff some of our programs based on the "Five Years Older" plan, then training of the staff members becomes even more important. We will need to emphasize appropriate interpersonal boundaries between campers and staffers. We will need to teach staffers appropriate leadership skills, methods of nurture and affirmation, as well as helpful methods of discipline.

Staffing our camping ministries presents some special considerations; but, none of them needs to be an insurmountable challenge. Careful screening and thorough training should enable our camping ministries to continue providing irreplaceable experiences of community, interdependence, leadership development, and faith building for children, youth, and adults.

Use of Criminal Background Checks

Including the use of criminal background checks or records checks as a part of the local church's recruiting/screening/hiring process for workers with children and youth is, without a doubt, the part of the process that is most often objected to. People seeking employment, or people who are simply volunteering to teach Sunday School, may say this is an invasion of their privacy and an affront to their integrity. Nevertheless, criminal background checks are an integral part of an adequate and diligent selection process.

Over the past decade, we have learned quite a bit about how criminal background checks can assist in the selection process. Today, every state has statutes that have created a sex offender registry website and requires all convicted sex offenders who are released on probation or parole to be registered on the website. Thus, when your church conducts a criminal background check on an applicant, the possibility exists that the report will come back showing the applicant has a conviction for a sexual offense. In addition, you can check the state sex offender registry website to get additional information, such as the offender's residence address. Access to these websites is free and instantaneous; however, it is important not to rely solely on them rather than a more complete background check. Each state has its own rules for how information if added to the sex offender registry and there is often significant delay between the offender's release from prison and his or her appearance on the website. The databases from which information is gathered in criminal background checks are more likely to be updated frequently.

It is often mentioned that many sex offenders who abuse children have many, many victims before they are ever reported or convicted of these offenses. In other words, you might conduct a criminal background check on an applicant who is, in fact, a child abuser, but the result will not

Notes:

_____

_____

_____

_____

_____

_____

_____

_____

_____

_____

_____

_____

_____

Notes: _____

_____

_____

_____

_____

_____

_____

_____

_____

_____

_____

_____

_____

show any convictions because he or she has never been caught. Does that mean conducting the criminal background checks is irrelevant? Certainly not. If the result of the background check shows no convictions and the applicant is hired, then later if he or she is accused of harming a child, the church will be able to show that it took reasonable screening steps, including the background check, before hiring this particular worker.

In spite of all we have learned about the value and importance of using criminal background checks as part of our selection process, comments will still be made, including, "I've been a member of this church for fifteen years, and if they don't trust me by now, they can just find someone else to keep the nursery!" Or, "What is this world coming to? All I wanted to do was help with Sunday school. What's the big deal?"

Nevertheless, criminal background checks have become a standard screening tool in churches. **Many states now require such inquiries by any organization recruiting workers with children as part of the state's child abuse laws.** Many churches make the decision to include this tool, even if not required by state law, as another way of reducing the probability that a selected worker has a history of child abuse.

The local church must decide what to do with the information it receives from background screening reports. A strict plan should be developed to ensure that information will be kept confidential and that it will only be shared with those who must know. Decisions will need to be made as to where the reports will be stored. Some churches today are arranging for online storage of all the screening documents. Many keep these documents in locked and confidential filing cabinets.

If information shows that an applicant was convicted of child abuse, child molestation, incest, or some other crime against a child, that applicant should definitely be rejected as a worker with children or youth. If information indicates that charges were filed against an applicant but that there was no conviction, then the church should investigate how the issue was resolved. Contact the police department or the prosecuting attorney's office to discover more of the details. When the maximum amount of information has

been gathered, you will need to make a decision about whether this applicant poses too great a risk to the church's children and youth. If any applicant voluntarily discloses to the pastor or the Safe Sanctuary selection committee a prior conviction for a charge of any type of child abuse, then that applicant should not be selected to work with children or youth. Be sure to document in the church's confidential file every step taken during the investigation and the decisions made.

No amount of resistance, objection, or lack of cooperation should stop a local congregation from developing and implementing comprehensive recruiting/screening/hiring policies and procedures for all its workers—paid or volunteer, clergy or lay, full-time or part-time—with children and youth. If any stranger or new member can have immediate access to our children, the effect of other safety procedures will be limited.

Notes: _____

_____

_____

_____

_____

_____

_____

_____

_____

_____

_____

_____

_____

_____

Part Two: Children

The Scope
of the Problem

EACH WEEK many local churches participate in the sacrament of Holy Baptism for children. In the congregation where I worship, we have two worship services each Sunday, and we very often have a baptism in each service. On a recent Sunday, we baptized a baby boy who represents the sixth generation of his family in our congregation. Can you imagine how that looked in the sanctuary? His parent, grandparents, and great-grandparents presented him for baptism. They, along with aunts, uncles, and cousins filled up the chancel area! Then, when our pastor presented him to the congregation, we all joined in by pledging to surround him and his family with steadfast love so that he would grow in the way that leads to eternal life surrounded by a community of faith that would love and care for him and his whole family. That was a worship-filled time; but not simply because we baptized a new baby. It was worship filled also because over the years, members of the baby's family had raised their voices in support of other families at the baptism and confirmation of their children and now, the tradition was being continued for them and their newest family member. All of us who belong to the community of faith rejoice at every event like this and hope that we will see many many more.

For each baptism, our pastor begins the service by reading Jesus' words, "Let the little children come to me, and do not stop them; for it is to such as these that the kingdom of heaven belongs" (Matthew 19:14). The parents and the congregation are examined as to their willingness to raise the child(ren) in the way that leads to faith, the child is named and baptized, and then the child is presented to the congregation. At this point, the congregation assumes a holy responsibility as it replies, "With God's help we will so order our lives after the example of Christ, that this child, surrounded by steadfast love, may be established in the faith, and confirmed and strengthened in the way that leads to life eternal"(The United Methodist Hymnal, p. 44). By our pledge, we commit to lead the child, by the example of our lives, into a life of Christian faith. By our pledge, we commit to support the parents in their efforts to lead their child into a life of Christian faith. By our pledge,

Notes: _____

_____

_____

_____

_____

_____

_____

_____

_____

_____

_____

_____

_____

Whoever Welcomes One
such child in my name
welcomes me.

Matthew 18:5

we vow to keep our church a holy place in which all children may come to know God and experience the love of Jesus Christ. When we think seriously about the promise we make in the baptismal service, we can only conclude that we are truly called to prevent child abuse in our churches. A friend of mine once shared a story with me about the baptism of an infant in her congregation. A mother of a newborn infant brought her forward for baptism. When the pastor presented her to the congregation, he introduced her; but before calling on the congregation to make the congregational pledge, he admonished them saying, "This young mother has brought her daughter for baptism today. She is a single mother. This baby is not going to grow up in a traditional two parent and two child family. She is going to grow up in our family—our church family. She and her mom are depending on you to live up to the responsibilities you pledge. So, if you can't live up to the responsibility of surrounding them with love, then don't make the pledge today. If you do make the pledge, make it with the assurance in your heart that you will, along with the rest of us, keep up with your duties toward this child."

This call to the congregation is a strong reminder that children, youth, and their families need the community of faith today more than ever. For many, the congregation will be the primary source for learning relationships of respect, integrity, compassion, and honor. Thus, more than ever, our congregations must be Safe Sanctuary congregations, where children and youth can rest assured that the ministries we provide will be staffed by trustworthy workers and operated in ways that will reduce the possibilities of abuse.

Anyone who reads newspapers, watches television, or listens to the radio knows that child abuse and violence against children happen all too frequently in our society. Each day brings another tragic story. The reports range from allegations of sexual abuse to allegations of inappropriate forms of punishment. Recently, I kept track of alleged incidents reported by the media. In just two weeks, there were reports including: the sexual molestation of middle school students by a trusted teacher; the sexual abuse of a teenage boy by a drifter already on probation for the sexual molestation of a minor; the sexual molestation of a preschooler by her stepfather; the pornographic exploitation of a preschooler by her parents, who offered the child to acquaintances in exchange for cocaine; and the sexual abuse of a preschooler by a Sunday school teacher. The abuse happened not in dark, isolated alleys but in the child's home, the child's daycare center, the child's school classroom, the child's summer camp, and the child's church. The identities of the alleged abusers ranged from parents, to aunts and uncles, to family friends, to teachers, to childcare workers, to camp counselors, to Sunday school teachers, to complete strangers. Today, according to the Center for Missing and Exploited Children (www.missingkids.com), one in every five children under 18 will be solicited for sex acts online.

No matter where a child is harmed or by whom, as Christians we grieve for the inestimable injury done and for the losses experienced by the child and the child's family. As Christians, we are called to move beyond grieving to active efforts to eliminate the possibility of child abuse everywhere, and most especially in our churches. Our churches need to be the safest and holiest of places for all children if we are to succeed in our efforts to make the gospel real in the lives of people in need.

The depth and breadth of the problem of child abuse is far greater than can be thoroughly addressed within this single resource. Today, ten years after the first publication of *Safe Sanctuaries*, it is sad that we must admit that we know the truth of this statement even more completely now than we did then. In spite of all the work of so many volunteers and staff members, congregations and conferences, we are still aware that abuse continues to occur and children and youth continue to be injured. We have learned that abuse is able to occur within ministries when we fail to select workers carefully and when we fail to carry out the programs and ministries with safety in mind. We have learned that the abuse of children and youth that we will be most often concerned with is not "stranger danger." Instead, it is abuse that is perpetrated by someone the child victim already knows and trusts and probably depends on. Reports show that more than 80% of child abuse is perpetuated by adults who already have a relationship with the child.

Types of Child Abuse

Generally, child abuse is categorized in five primary forms: physical abuse, emotional abuse, neglect, sexual abuse, and ritual abuse.

1. Physical Abuse

Abuse in which a person deliberately and intentionally causes bodily harm to a child. Examples may include violent battery with a weapon (knife, belt, strap, and so

Notes: _____
_____
_____
_____
_____
_____
_____
_____
_____
_____
_____
_____
_____

WHAT IS ABUSE?
Child abuse may include
- Physical Abuse
- Emotional Abuse
- Neglect
- Sexual Abuse
- Ritual Abuse

Notes: _____

_____

_____

_____

_____

_____

_____

_____

_____

_____

_____

_____

_____

THE CHILD VICTIM IS NEVER
responsible for causing the abuse, and the child victim is never to be blamed for the abuse.

forth), burning, shaking, kicking, choking, fracturing bones, and any of a wide variety of non-accidental injuries to a child's body.

2. Emotional Abuse

Abuse in which a person exposes a child to spoken and/or unspoken violence or emotional cruelty. Emotional abuse sends a message to the child of worthlessness, badness, and being not only unloved but undeserving of love and care. Children exposed to emotional abuse may have experienced being locked in a closet, being deprived of any sign of parental affection, being constantly told they are bad or stupid, or being allowed or forced to abuse alcohol or drugs. Emotional abuse is often very difficult to prove and is devastating to the victim.

3. Neglect

Abuse in which a person endangers a child's health, safety, or welfare through negligence. Neglect may include withholding food, clothing, medical care, education, and even affection and affirmation of the child's self-worth. This is perhaps the most common form of abuse.

4. Sexual Abuse

Abuse in which sexual contact between a child and an adult (or another older and more powerful youth) occurs. The child is never truly capable of consenting to or resisting such contact and/or such sexual acts. Often, the child is physically and psychologically dependent upon the perpetrator of the abuse. Examples of sexual abuse may include fondling, intercourse, incest, and the exploitation of and exposure to child pornography or prostitution.

5. Ritual Abuse

Abuse in which physical, sexual, or psychological violations of a child are inflicted regularly, intentionally, and in a stylized way by a person or persons responsible for the child's welfare. The abuser may appeal to some higher authority or power to justify the abuse. The abuse may include cruel treatment of animals or repeated threats of harm to the child, other persons, and animals. Reports of ritual abuse are often extremely horrifying and may seem too grim to be true. Children making such reports must not be ignored.

It Can Happen Anywhere

When a child reports that he or she has experienced the behaviors detailed in these descriptions, serious attention should be paid to the report. While not every child's story is actually a report of abuse, the truth needs to be determined to prevent either further harm to the child or further false allegations.

Child abuse is criminal behavior and is punished severely in every state. Although each state has its own specific legal definition, generally speaking, child sexual abuse exploits and harms children by involving them in sexual behavior for which they are unprepared, to which they cannot consent, and from which they are unable to protect themselves. Every state in the United States defines sexual contact between children and adults as criminal behavior.

The child victim is **never responsible** for causing the abuse, and the child victim is **never to be blamed** for the abuse. The child victim is **never capable of consent to abusive behavior**, either legally or morally. Child sexual abuse is **always** wrong and is solely the responsibility of the abuser.

Once, while teaching in a continuing education event for clergy, I was asked this question, "If the American Psychiatric Association removes pedophilia from the DSM–IV (*The Diagnostic and Statistical Manual of Mental Disorders*, 4th ed.) as a diagnosed mental disease, will you stop using pedophilia as an example of child sexual abuse in the classes that you teach?" My answer was an emphatic "No, because all fifty state governments define sexual contact between adults and children as criminal behavior; therefore, until all fifty states change their statutory definitions of child sexual abuse, I will continue to use this type of example." The current state of our laws on this matter is that children are not legally capable of giving meaningful consent to sexual contact from an adult; therefore, such behavior is always wrong and is always abuse.

The church must and certainly can work to assure children and families that abuse of children will not be tolerated or ignored in the community of faith. The church can demonstrate its commitment to provide a safe, secure place where all children can grow in faith and wisdom by seriously addressing the need to develop and implement abuse prevention policies and strategies for every congregation.

Notes: _____

_____

_____

_____

_____

_____

_____

_____

_____

_____

_____

THREE MILLION INCIDENTS OF child abuse are reported each year. That equates to one incident every 10 seconds around the clock, seven days a week!

Notes: _____

_____

_____

_____

_____

_____

_____

_____

_____

_____

_____

_____

_____

SEXUAL CONTACT BETWEEN
an adult and a child is defined in all fifty states as child sexual abuse and punishable as criminal behavior.

Frequently, when congregations are first considering the task of developing a child abuse prevention policy and strategy, one or more members may respond: "Well, this is silly. Such an awful thing would never happen in our church!" Or, "I think we're blowing this issue out of proportion—just because it happens in the big city churches doesn't mean it would ever happen here." Or, "We have a hard enough time recruiting volunteers for Sunday school and keeping the nursery. If we start making each worker answer a lot of questions and sign a covenant we'll scare everybody off— then what will we do?" Or, "I don't see much point in this since we don't have any children in this church."

These comments reflect not only our reluctance to admit that the horrors of child abuse are real for a large number of children, but they also reflect our complete abhorrence of the thought that such crimes could happen in our churches—our very holiest of places! Perhaps comments like these reveal our confidence that in "our church" atrocities cannot happen. These responses are usually made by individuals who are unfailingly optimistic or dangerously naïve. I think of them collectively as the "Yes, buts . . .". Let me give you a couple of examples of how the "Yes, buts" can be transformed into the "Yes, ands"—those who realize that child abuse can happen anywhere, anytime, and that we, in our congregations, really can do a lot to reduce the chances of it happening within our ministries. There is a small church in my annual conference that had no children or youth in the congregation when our conference adopted a Safe Sanctuaries policy. The lay leader of the church contacted the conference staff person who had responsibility for children's ministries. She asked, "If we have no children or youth, do we really have to develop a Safe Sanctuaries policy?" In other words, she was saying that even though preventing child abuse was a good concept, her congregation didn't need to think about it because the average member there was sixty years old! Our conference staff member listened to her and then replied, "Well, if you don't have *any* children or youth, and you don't think you ever will, then I suppose you don't have to develop a Safe Sanctuaries policy and procedures. But, don't you *want* some children?" That question transformed the lay leader's thinking. She led the church council in developing Safe Sanctuary policies and procedures that were simple and practical and could be implemented easily when her grandchild, or any other member's grandchild visited during the summer. Then, the church council members began thinking beyond that first vision. Realizing that they needed younger members if the congregation was to continue as a viable community of faith, they got to work. The lay leader and the pastor called the local newspaper. A reporter interviewed them and ran a feature story about the congregation's new Safe Sanctuaries policies and their desire to invite families with children and youth to attend worship and Sunday School. This congregation transformed the burden of developing Safe Sanctuaries procedures into a vital tool for evangelism in the community. The "Yes, buts . . ." became devoted "Yes, ands . . ."

In another church in my annual conference, the "Yes, buts" told the pastor, "We can't do Safe Sanctuaries because we don't have enough adults to put two in every class. Those members didn't know some things that the pastor knew. There was one member who was a survivor of child sexual abuse perpetrated by the pastor of the church she attended as a child. Furthermore, the pastor and that member knew that the abusive pastor had recently moved into their local community. Together, they worked on plans to staff every children's class with two adults, and if they couldn't find two for each teaching team, they provided a "roaming helper", so that any one teaching alone on any date would have the assistance and supervision of another adult dropping in during the class to help with crafts, or snacks, or whatever was needed. It didn't take long for the "Yes, buts" to begin to see that there were more volunteers coming forward than they had expected.

The member and the pastor were grateful for the volunteers who were there; but the member had another goal. She wanted to do what she could to invite the children from the community to her church, so that they and their families would not be put at risk the way she had been as a child. With the permission of the pastor and the church council, she had bookmarks made and laminated to place in the hymnals and pew Bibles with the congregation's Safe Sanctuaries policies printed on them. As soon as she had put the bookmarks in every hymnal, she took the leftovers (she had several thousand printed!) to the merchants downtown in that community. Every merchant she approached allowed her to put a box of the bookmarks at the check-out counter to be given away free to any customer who wanted one. She and the pastor saw the bookmark give away as an outreach tool, and they were right. By announcing the Safe Sanctuaries commitment of the congregation in the businesses of the community, they were able to let newcomers know where they and their

Notes:

_____

_____

_____

_____

_____

_____

_____

_____

_____

_____

_____

_____

WHILE A CHURCH CANNOT guarantee the safety of every person, every church can be responsible for reducing the circumstances that could lead to harm or injury.

Notes: _____

_____

_____

_____

_____

_____

_____

_____

_____

_____

_____

_____

_____

WHO ARE ABUSERS?

Abusers are not easily recognizable –they may look just like you or me! Abusers are people who have greater power in relation to a child, and they use that power to harm the child.

children would be welcomed. The "Yes, buts" were surprised and happy when visitors began to join more and more frequently.

Before their work in devising abuse prevention strategies is complete, members will inevitably learn that no church is immune from the horrors of child abuse simply because it wishes to be. During the course of their work, they may hear about an incident in the church across the street; or a member of the congregation will reveal that he or she is a survivor of childhood abuse and is grateful that the congregation is taking this task so seriously; or a child's parent will report a suspected incident of abuse to the pastor. Without a doubt, the congregation's work will take on a new and deeper sense of importance when revelations from "close to home" are made known.

Knowing the Facts

When child abuse occurs in our own neighborhoods, it gets our attention and sometimes serves as a catalyst in a way that nameless and faceless children counted in statistics cannot. However, it is important to be familiar with a few statistics:

- The National Center for Child Abuse and Neglect reports that there are more than three million incidents of physical abuse and/or neglect per year in the United States of America. That equates to more than thirty out of every one thousand children.
- Studies have estimated that 1 out of 3 girls is sexually abused before the age of 18. Similarly, studies indicate 1 out of 7 boys have been sexually abused before the age of 18. Even more frightening is that these numbers may be underestimated since many children are reluctant to report abuse.
- The National Committee for the Prevention of Child Abuse in the United States reports that at least 1,490 deaths attributable to child abuse and/or neglect occur each year.

Let's think again about the first number listed: three million incidents of abuse per year. That equals 8,219 children abused each day; approximately 343 children abused per hour; nearly 6 (5.7) children abused per minute; and one child abused every 10 seconds, night or day, weekday or weekend, including Sundays!

The Church at Risk

In light of the statistics, it seems that any organization involved with children and youth is a place where abuse could occur. What makes the risk for churches especially high? Several factors must be included in our analysis:

- Churches behave as relatively trusting organizations, relying upon their members and their leaders to conduct themselves appropriately. Too often, this trusting attitude persists even in the face of questions or reports of misconduct. The truth is that more than 85% percent of the reported incidents of abuse are perpetrated by an individual that the child already knows and trusts, including persons in the church.
- Churches are notoriously inactive when it comes to screening volunteers and/or employees who work with children and youth. Too often, no application is used and no references are checked at all before a total stranger is welcomed aboard.
- Churches routinely provide opportunities for close contact and for close personal relationships with children and youth. Indeed, they are nurtured and encouraged as we try to live out the gospel message.

Simultaneously with the growth of the church's need for greater numbers of workers with children and youth, there has been an explosion in litigation against the church for incidents of child sexual abuse. Every state now has some statutory requirements in place for the reporting of an incident of child abuse. This, coupled with the blazing attention focused by the media on the child victim and the church, has increased the number of criminal charges against the perpetrators of abuse and the number of civil lawsuits seeking monetary damages for the injuries suffered by the child.

The concept of *"charitable immunity,"* which in the past shielded churches from many types of litigation, no longer serves as a viable protection in cases of child abuse. The public and the courts deem the harm done by child abuse too great to allow such incidents to go unreported and unpunished. Frequently, the punishment comes in the form of monetary damages in huge verdicts against the perpetrator and/or the institution in which the perpetrator worked or volunteered. While a church cannot be the absolute guarantor of the safety of each person within its community and its ministries, it must be recognized that every church can be responsibly attentive to reducing and eliminating

Notes: _____

_____

_____

_____

_____

_____

_____

_____

_____

_____

_____

_____

_____

Less Than Twenty Percent
of child abuse is perpetrated by strangers.

Notes: _____

_____

_____

_____

_____

_____

_____

_____

_____

_____

_____

_____

WITHOUT A COMPREHENSIVE strategy against abuse, we are taking a needless risk that harm may be done to our children or our workers with children.

circumstances that could in some situations lead to harm or injury. Nearly every day the news media reports more cases of huge settlements or verdicts against churches or church-related institutions in cases of child abuse. One recent case, involving a church camp, resulted in a settlement exceeding a million dollars for the two victims. The camp had very limited insurance coverage and other resources with which to pay the settlement. Thus, the annual conference had to step in, along with the local churches in the annual conference, to provide the funding of the settlement. In another recent case, the claims of three victims against two annual conferences and two local churches were settled in an amount exceeding five million dollars. Settlements or verdicts of this size are staggering to local churches, camps, schools, and denominations. It is not an overstatement to say that cases like these have the potential to bankrupt our ministries financially and spiritually.

Recognizing the frequency of the occurrence of child abuse is only part of the task. As a church, we must become knowledgeable about how to recognize indicators of possible abuse, and we must become knowledgeable about how to safely carry out our ministries without at the same time providing opportunities for abusers to harm our children.

The church must not look upon the reality of child abuse as a reason to withdraw from its ministries with children! Instead, we must work to assure that our ministries are carried out in responsibly safe circumstances. We, as members of the community of faith, are called to remember the pledge made as each child is baptized. Remembering that, we are called to make the church a safe and holy place where children will be confirmed and strengthened in their faith.

Indicators of Child Abuse

Children suffering abuse often will not tell anyone about it. Therefore, it is important to be able to recognize other signs of abuse. The following characteristics may be indicators of abuse, although they are not necessarily proof. Individually, any one of the indicators may be signs of a number of other more or less serious problems. When these indicators are observed in a child, they can be considered as warnings and lead you to look into the situation further.

Possible Signs of Physical Abuse
1. Hostile and aggressive behavior toward others
2. Fearfulness of parents and/or other adults

3. Destructive behavior toward self, others, and/or property
4. Inexplicable fractures or bruises inappropriate for child's developmental stage
5. Burns, facial injuries, pattern of repetitious bruises

Possible Signs of Emotional Abuse
1. Exhibits severe depression and/or withdrawal
2. Exhibits severe lack of self-esteem
3. Failure to thrive
4. Threatens or attempts suicide
5. Speech and/or eating disorders
6. Goes to extremes to seek adult approval
7. Extreme passive/aggressive behavior patterns

Possible Signs of Neglect
1. Failure to thrive
2. Pattern of inappropriate dress for climate
3. Begs or steals food; chronic hunger
4. Depression
5. Untreated medical conditions
6. Poor hygiene

Possible Signs of Sexual Abuse
1. Unusually advanced sexual knowledge and/or behavior for child's age and developmental stage
2. Depression—cries often for no apparent reason
3. Promiscuous behavior
4. Runs away from home and refuses to return
5. Difficulty walking or sitting
6. Bruised/bleeding in vaginal or anal areas
7. Exhibits frequent headaches, stomachaches, extreme fatigue
8. Sexually transmitted diseases

In addition to these indicators, children who have been sexually abused at church may exhibit some of the following:
1. Unusual nervousness or anxiety about being left in the nursery or Sunday school class
2. Reluctance to participate in church activities that were previously enthusiastically approached
3. Comments such as "I don't want to be alone with _____" in reference to a childcare worker or Sunday school teacher
4. Nightmares including a childcare worker or teacher as a frightening character
5. Unexplained hostility toward a childcare worker or teacher

Notes: _____
_____
_____
_____
_____
_____
_____
_____
_____
_____
_____
_____
_____
_____
_____

CHILD ABUSE IN THE CHURCH
creates many victims:
- the child
- the child's family
- the congregation
- the family of the abuser

Notes: _____

_____

_____

_____

_____

_____

_____

_____

_____

_____

_____

_____

Possible Signs of Ritual Abuse
1. Disruptions of memory or consciousness
2. Unexplained mistrust and mood swings
3. Flashbacks
4. Eating disorders
5. Fear of the dark, especially at sundown or a full moon
6. Agitation or despair that seems to occur in cycles
7. Fear of ministers, priests, or others wearing robes or uniforms
8. Nightmares or sleep disorders
9. Any of the symptoms of sexual abuse

Child abuse occurs every minute of every day, and it occurs in every community. Child abuse occurs in every economic, racial, ethnic, religious, or other demographic group. No segment of our society is immune. As Christians, we are called to be vigilant in protecting the children in our midst and in preventing child abuse in the community of faith.

Abusers: Who Are They?

To prevent child abuse in our churches, we must not only recognize the signs of abuse, but we must recognize that the abusers of our children are more often than not familiar adults trusted by the children.

Just as children from all segments of our society are victims of child sexual abuse, it is also true that abusers come from all segments of society. Abusers can be found in every racial, ethnic, economic, and social group. When they are identified, they look very much like us. Some are charismatic leaders; some are very sociable; some are very sympathetic to troubled children; some are married and have children; some are young (even as young as fourteen or fifteen); and some are older adults. More than sixty percent of child abusers who are caught abuse again. It is common for the child abuser to have dozens and dozens of victims.

Minor on Minor Misconduct and Abuse

A growing area of concern for ministries with children and youth is misconduct between two, or more, children or youth. There is increasing media attention being given to school situations in which one student injures another. Although similar situations in churches may be infrequent, they certainly exist. The number of claims being made against churches for misconduct of minors has increased over the past few years. Some insurance companies are finding that approximately 20% of the claims received are for situations involving minors as the perpetrators of abuse or violence.

There are several different types of situations that can lead to abuse between minors. The first could be a situation in which one minor is in a position of power over another. For example, a case might involve a male fourth grade student who is physically almost double the weight of a female third grade student and he uses his size advantage to coerce her and to injure her repeatedly over a period of weeks. She reports his behavior to her teacher and to her parents; but nothing is done to protect her after the first report. She continues to report the misconduct to her teacher and her parents. Finally, her parents remove her from the school because they can find no other way to assure her safety from continued assaults.

Another type of occurrence could be described as some sort of a practical joke between two or more minors. This type of behavior might start out as simply one child or youth using words with sexually charged connotations to embarrass or humiliate another. In the past, these sorts of "jokes" created more than enough embarrassment for the one victim who was targeted by the one initiator. In today's world, when such a thing is broadcast over the internet through email, blogs, websites, and text messages, the painful effect is exponentially magnified for the victim.

Finally, we know that sexual activity between minors is commonplace. However, the frequency with which it occurs does not make this behavior always consensual or acceptable. All fifty states have statutes defining the terms in which sexual contact between persons is criminal. Most states find sexual contact with a minor who is more than four years younger than the adult to be criminal behavior. Similarly, sexual contact between minors who are more than four years apart in age is defined as criminal conduct.

Within the Church

Within our churches, who are the abusers? They may be Sunday School teachers, nursery workers, preschool teachers, children's choir helpers, vacation Bible school leaders, camp counselors, youth group counselors, clergy persons, or anyone else. Today, many congregations are having an experience they haven't had before regarding their interactions with child abusers. When a convicted sex offender who has been probated or paroled approaches the pastor and asks to "join" the church, telling the pastor that he

Notes: _____

_____

_____

_____

_____

_____

_____

_____

_____

_____

_____

Notes: _____

_____

_____

_____

_____

_____

_____

_____

_____

_____

_____

_____

_____

wants to participate in order to grow in faith, the pastor must know the requirements of state law regarding where convicted offenders may live, work, and volunteer.

In the past, there were no laws regulating these issues, or the laws were less stringent. Now, our states have enacted statutes requiring the convicted offenders who are being probated to register with the law enforcement authorities of the county in which they want to reside. Furthermore, many of these statutes restrict offenders from living, working, or "being found" within a certain distance from any location where children may be found. Some of the statutes make the distance as little as one thousand feet. Some of the state statutes make an exception to allow convicted offenders to attend worship in a church; however, that exception does not extend to allowing the offender to participate as a volunteer or employee of the church. In many cases, the offender also has additional requirements of probation that impact where he can live, work, and volunteer. Thus, when an offender approaches the pastor about participating in the congregation, the first thing the pastor needs to do is make contact with the individual's probation/ parole officer and find out whether or not participating in worship, or in other church activities, would be a probation violation.

The 2004 Book of Resolutions for the United Methodist Church includes a resolution giving a reasonable and practical approach to dealing with the safety concerns for the congregation as well as the offender. (See p. 102.)

How Does Abuse Happen?

Child sexual abuse happens when a person exerts his or her power over a child in ways that harm and/or exploit the child. In other words, the abuser is powerful; the child is vulnerable. There may be several sources from which the abuser gains power over the child: size, position, knowledge, money, just to name a few. All of these things work to make the abuser believe that he or she is able to behave inappropriately toward a child and that the child will be unable to stop the abusive behavior.

The child is vulnerable to an abuser as a result of having fewer resources available to him or her. The child is physically smaller and weaker, intellectually less mature, and economically dependent upon the abuser or some other adult for sustenance. When a child's vulnerability and an

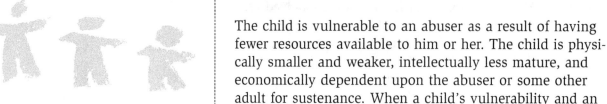

abuser's misuse of power combine with the opportunity to exploit the child without being discovered, then child sexual abuse may and often does occur. Therefore, by designing ministries that minimize opportunities for isolation and secrecy we will reduce the possibilities of abuse.

Members of our churches do not like to think that any person in the Sunday school or any other ministry of the church would harm a child. Conversely, we do not like to think that false allegations of abuse could be made by any child in the church. Without a comprehensive strategy against abuse, we are taking a needless risk that harm may be done to our children or our workers with children.

It is imperative for our churches **not** to adopt or implement child abuse prevention policies that apply to only a few categories of people. Strategies must be supported by the whole congregation and carried out by applying the same policies and requirements to each worker involved in children and youth ministries. When a congregation adopts a Safe Sanctuaries strategy that applies only to the paid nursery workers or only to professional staff members, it has adopted a plan that is doomed to be no more than partially successful. Such an imcomplete plan exempts many people from the strategy's requirements and may create specific opportunities for abusers to have unlimited access to our children.

Consequences of Child Sexual Abuse

When one child is sexually abused within our church, many victims are created, including the child, the congregation, the child's family, and often the family of the abuser.

Of foremost importance is the child who has been harmed; he or she must be cared for. Innocence has been stolen from the child. The trauma of abuse may cause emotional injury as well as physical injury, and these scars may last through the victim's life. When child sexual abuse is perpetrated by a trusted person in the church, even greater harm is done to the child's faith in God and faith in the church. The child may struggle with questions like: "If God loves children, how could God have let this happen to me?" and "How can the members of this congregation continue praying and singing week after week, acting as if nothing has happened?" Experiences of abuse in the church create massive obstacles to the child's development of a living, sustaining faith. This consequence is no less important

Notes: _____

_____

_____

_____

_____

_____

_____

_____

_____

_____

_____

_____

Notes: _____

_____

_____

_____

_____

_____

_____

_____

_____

_____

_____

_____

than the physical injuries or the eventual depression, fear, and lack of sufficient self-esteem that often develop as a result of sexual abuse.

The congregation also becomes a victim after abuse is revealed. Members are stunned that such a crime could have been perpetrated within their midst. They are humiliated at their failure to maintain the church as a safe and holy place for children. Members fear that they are ill-equipped to help the child's healing process. They are angry that a person welcomed into their fellowship would dare to violate the gospel's mandate by harming a child. Often, members are divided when the congregation begins to think about how to address all of the problems created by the incident.

In addition, the congregation may suffer for a very long time if civil or criminal litigation ensues as a result of the abuse. Litigation in the courts keeps the incident alive for an extended period of time and may make resolution of the emotional issues even more difficult. Over the past decade, litigation involving congregations has become more frequent. As a result, we are finally becoming aware of the effects on the congregation of the long, time-consuming, and costly process. **Although criminal or civil litigation is often necessary in such situations, the litigation process itself will not provide what is needed for healing among the congregation's members.** For this healing, the community of faith must delve into its biblical foundations and find strength to conquer the evils of fear as well as to conquer the lack of knowledge about abuse. The congregation must make a renewed commitment to living out the gospel's call to provide and care for children. The spouse and children of an accused abuser may also be harmed when the allegations become known. In the event the accused is convicted, the spouse and children may be left without income and without a home. They may also be embarrassed and frightened.

Finally, the financial consequences of child sexual abuse in the church cannot be ignored. As reports of abuse and lawsuits increase, the financial costs rise exponentially. A victim of child sexual abuse and his or her family will suffer financially since the costs of counseling and medical treatment go higher each year. A congregation need only ask its insurance company for the latest information to learn that the amounts paid by churches, as settlements or verdicts in abuse cases, can be astronomical—ranging from many

thousands of dollars to many millions. A recent study, conducted by Prevent Child Abuse America, estimated the annual costs of child abuse in the United States in 2000 exceeded ninety-six billion dollars. That amount did not include the amounts paid in settlements or verdicts in church related cases. That amount rivals the budget appropriation amount in 2004 of the United States Department of Defense for funding the war in Iraq.

Currently, no congregation can afford, either financially, ethically, or morally, to fail to implement strategies for the reduction and prevention of child sexual abuse. We, as Christians, are not called to discontinue our congregations' ministries with children and youth. We are called to engage in these ministries with great rejoicing and with the knowledge that we are making every effort to provide ministry to our children and youth in ways that assure their safety while they grow in faith.

Notes: _____

_____

_____

_____

_____

_____

_____

_____

_____

_____

_____

_____

_____

Basic Procedures for Safe Ministry with Children

AFTER A LOCAL CHURCH has made the commitment to take precautions against abuse in its ministries with children and youth, the congregation needs to develop basic procedures to guide the day-to-day operation of its ministries. This can be thought of as the "nuts and bolts" of carrying out the church's ministries with children after the workers are chosen. These procedures are designed to make ministry flow smoothly by reducing the possibility of harm to the children, youth, and the workers. Once again, the procedures will demonstrate to members and visitors alike the church's commitment to the prevention of child abuse and its commitment to being a safe and holy place where children can grow in the faith.

Each of the following procedures is important in the congregation's comprehensive prevention strategy. They are not listed in order of importance.

The "Two-Adult Rule"

Simply stated, the "Two-Adult Rule" requires no fewer than two adults present at all times during any church-sponsored program, event, or ministry involving children. Risk will be reduced even more if the two adults are not related. The nursery is always attended by at least two adults. A Sunday school class for children is always led by at least two adults. A Bible study group for youth is always taught by at least two adults. The youth fellowship group is always staffed with at least two adult counselors/leaders.

The significance of this rule cannot be overstated. A church will drastically reduce the possibility of an incident of child abuse if this rule is followed. **Abusers thrive on secrecy, isolation, and their ability to manipulate victims. When abusers know they will never have a chance to be alone with potential victims, they quickly lose interest in "working" with the children.** Thus, the children are protected, and the church has greatly reduced

Notes: _____

_____

_____

_____

_____

_____

_____

_____

_____

_____

_____

A Church Will Drastically
reduce the possibility of an incident of child abuse by following the "Two-Adult" rule.

the likelihood of an allegation of child abuse. Furthermore, vigilant adherence to the "Two-Adult Rule" provides important protection to the church's workers with children and youth. Even small churches can adhere to this rule by using assigned adult "roamers" who move in and out of rooms. Parents and children who know that two adults will be present at all times are less likely to make false allegations; they know that it would be nearly impossible to prove allegations against two workers. Church members will be more confident when they volunteer to work with children, knowing that they will never bear the total burden of leadership and knowing that the church has made a commitment to protecting them as well as the children.

First Aid/CPR Training
Providing first aid and CPR training on an annual basis for all church workers with children and youth is a basic step to assure the safety of children. It is hoped that first aid or CPR would never be needed in the church. Nevertheless, ministries with children and youth inevitably involve activities that can result in bumps, bruises, and scrapes. Having workers who are prepared to deal with these competently goes a long way toward building the confidence of the children and the parents involved in the ministry of the church.

Annual Orientation for Workers
All workers with children and youth, whether the workers are paid, volunteer, part-time, full-time, clergy, or lay, should be required to attend an orientation session in which they are informed of the

- church's policies for the prevention of child abuse.
- procedures to be used in all ministries with children and youth.
- appropriate steps to report an incident of child abuse.
- details of the state laws regarding child abuse.

At this orientation and training, the workers are given a copy of the Safe Sanctuaries Participation Covenant statement. They are to sign the covenant to abide by and cooperate with the church's policies and procedures for Safe Sanctuaries. This will give the church an up-to-date record that it has informed all of its workers about its policies and procedures. Workers who do not attend should be contacted and given the opportunity to renew the covenant form.

In many churches, orientation for the workers with children and youth will need to be done more frequently than once a year because new workers are needed and recruited on a monthly or quarterly basis. Additionally, there may need to be occasional training and orientation for workers being recruited for special events such as retreats or mission trips.

The "Five-Years-Older" Rule

Often, especially in youth ministry, the people who volunteer to work or who apply for a paid position are in college or have just graduated. If a junior in college (age 20 or 21) is recruited to serve as a counselor in the senior-high youth fellowship, the counselor may be "leading" youth who are only three or four years younger than he or she is. This should be prohibited for the protection of the youth and the worker. Nearly every church has members who can remember a situation in which this rule was not followed and the persons involved came to regret it. Do not make the same mistake.

No Workers under the Age of Eighteen

When a church implements this rule it goes a long way toward reducing the risks of injuries to its children and youth. A very common practice in churches is to allow junior- and senior-high aged volunteers in the church nursery. In effect, the church is using children to supervise children. While in some situations they may provide excellent help, people under the age of eighteen cannot be expected to have developed the maturity and judgment that is needed to be fully responsible for younger children. It is also a common practice to use workers under the age of eighteen for staffing Vacation Bible school classes. Volunteer workers under the age of eighteen can be very helpful when placed as assistants in the classrooms, or on the playground, or in the gym, or in the music room. However, teenagers should not be assigned as the sole leaders or workers in any Vacation Bible school setting. An adult should always be assigned as the leader and teenagers assigned as helpers. **Putting children in charge of children invites problems.**

Windows in All Classroom Doors

Each room set aside for children and youth should have a door with a window in it or a half door. A window in every door removes the opportunity for secrecy and isolation, conditions every child abuser seeks. A half door offers protection against children wandering outside the classroom and allows for full visual access. Pastors today have added windows in their office doors in order to set a good example for churches and to protect themselves against false allegations of misconduct.

Notes: _____
_____
_____
_____
_____
_____
_____
_____
_____
_____
_____
_____
_____

A WINDOW IN EVERY DOOR

removes the opportunity for secrecy and isolation, conditions every child abuser seeks.

Notes: _____

_____

_____

_____

_____

_____

_____

_____

_____

_____

_____

_____

_____

PROVIDING PARENTS WITH
advanced notice and full
information about activities must
be a guiding principle in a church's
ministries with children.

Open-Door Counseling

At any counseling sessions with children or youth, the door of the room used should remain open for the entire session if the door has no window in it. Ideally, the session will be conducted at a time when others are nearby, even if they are not within listening distance. Counseling sessions conducted behind closed doors are a breeding ground for false allegations of abuse. Closed doors also make it too easy for the child abuser to have the privacy and isolation he or she needs. The youth minister's office in my church is set up very well for meeting with youth, or parents, safely. There is a window in the door so that whenever someone walks past the office, there is a clear view of who is in the office. However, with the door closed, the confidentiality of what is being said is preserved, without creating secrecy or isolation that could lead to difficulty.

Advance Notice to Parents

A basic rule for ministry with children and youth is to **always** give the parents advance notice and full information regarding the event(s) in which their children will be participating. Notify parents of any event in which a worker will be alone with a child. Before the event, parents must give written permission for their child's participation. Doing this protects the church in that it proves that parents were informed of the event, advised of the situation, and given the chance to prevent their child from being alone with a worker.

Providing parents with advance notice and full information about activities must be a guiding principle in a church's ministries with children and youth. Advance information encourages parents to support the ministry by scheduling their child's participation. It could also possibly lead to parents participating in the ministry as volunteer leaders. Advance information can help parents and children decide whether the content and substance of the event are suitable for their participation. Most important, advance information demonstrates that the church takes its ministries seriously enough to plan thoroughly and to provide for the safest possible experiences.

Participation Covenant for All Participants and Leaders

A written Safe Sanctuaries covenant of participation should be developed and provided to all leaders and participants in children's and youth ministries. The Safe Sanctuaries covenant is a statement in which the participants and leaders agree to

- take part in the ministry.
- give their best efforts to the ministry.
- respect the other participants.
- treat the others as well as they would wish to be treated.

Such Safe Sanctuaries covenants are useful (especially for retreats and trips) for establishing from the outset the behavior standards expected of everyone. Safe Sanctuaries covenants are also important reminders for leaders that abusive behavior toward the children will not be tolerated.

Parent and Family Education

When a church has made a serious commitment to a comprehensive plan for the prevention of child abuse within its ministries, it will want to provide information about the plan to the congregation and parents. A family education event, or a series of events, in which families are invited to learn the facts about child sexual abuse and about the components of the church's plan is highly effective in disseminating full information to the maximum number of people in a minimal amount of time. An event of this type could include:

- a speaker from your local law enforcement agency.
- a speaker from a local child protective services agency.
- a doctor or counselor who is experienced in treating abused children.
- an attorney experienced in advising churches about risk management or loss prevention.
- a video about the incidence of child sexual abuse within churches.
- printed information about your state's abuse statutes and abuse reporting requirements.
- printed copies of your church's abuse prevention policies and procedures. (Allow time for discussion.)
- a time for worship and prayer.

An event can also include sessions for children so that they are informed about the behavior that is to be expected from other participants and from church leaders, about how to recognize and report possible abuse, and about how they can help prevent harm being done to anyone at the church.

In a church committed to the prevention of child abuse within its ministries, these types of events will be provided

Notes:

_____

_____

_____

_____

_____

_____

_____

_____

_____

_____

_____

_____

_____

Planning for Their
physical safety is a necessary part of your ministry with children.

Notes: _____

_____

_____

_____

_____

_____

_____

_____

_____

_____

_____

_____

_____

regularly to accommodate new members and new parents. Just recently, the youth ministry team at my local church decided to host a new educational event for parents. The event's purpose was to educate parents about safety in "cyberspace" for children and youth. (For a broader discussion on appropriate cybersafety guidelines for churches, see p. 74 in the youth section.) This kind of educational opportunity, provided on a regular basis, will always be welcomed by parents.

Appropriate Equipment and Supervision

Ministries with children are carried out in an endless variety of settings and locations: church sanctuaries, classrooms, camp cabins, playgrounds, retreat centers, tour buses, parks, and homes. Reports of child abuse indicate that abuse happens in an equally large variety of settings. One aspect of planning for the safety of the children and youth participants is arranging for the ministry to take place in an appropriate setting. For instance, if the purpose of the ministry is weekly Bible study, then an appropriate setting would be a classroom at the church. If the purpose of the ministry is for the youth choir to travel for two weeks performing a musical in a dozen different cities, then the settings may include a tour bus, a series of hotel rooms, and a series of church sanctuaries.

The likelihood of the occurrence of child abuse varies in different settings and circumstances. Bible study done in an open-doored classroom and in the presence of no fewer than two adults has a very low probability of an incident happening. However, inadequate supervision of a youth choir at a hotel may increase the odds of an abuse incident. It is very important for those planning ministries with children and youth to think through, in advance, the advantages and disadvantages of the settings they are considering.

If the ministry involves the use of the church playground, then the workers should know how each piece of play equipment is to be used. When children are on the playground, an adequate number of adults should be with them at all times. Too often stories are told about abuse that occurred on a playground when only one adult (the abuser) was present and had a brief opportunity to isolate the victim out of the sight of anyone else. Incredible as it may seem, children are sometimes left totally unattended on the playground while a dinner or some other event goes on in the church's fellowship hall. A complete stranger can take advantage of the situation to hurt a child, or a child can fall and break an arm without a single adult present to see what happened or to attend to the injury. Both of these situations can lead to nightmarish legal consequences for the church. Do not let your church take this risk.

Other outdoor ministries would involve the need for specialized knowledge. Swimming or rafting events need a supervisor with lifeguard skills. When the ministry involves camping, hiking, and service projects such as Habitat for Humanity or the Appalachian Service Project, first aid and CPR skills are needed.

Camping

I am a camper, a camp counselor, the parent of a camper and a camp counselor, an educator for camp staffers, and an attorney for camps. My experiences in each of these roles have shown me the value of camping ministries. While the following is by no means comprehensive (indeed, entire books are written on camping ministries alone), it does provide a place to start.

Church related camps provide faith building opportunities that would be unavailable in many other settings. City dwelling children may have no better way to experience the outdoors and to learn good stewardship of our natural resources. Junior highs and senior highs may have opportunities to think about God's call for vocation, in small groups with leaders already dedicated to Christian vocations, that don't come easily in their local communities. Many campers find new confidence in themselves and in their abilities to cooperate, share, and contribute to the well-being of themselves and others.

When the camping experience is good for a camper, it can be wonderfully memorable. When the camping experience is not good, it can be the source of unhappiness, unpleasant memories, and litigation. Operating procedures are a key ingredient in assuring good experiences.

Here is an example of what I mean. We registered our daughter for camp during the first summer she was old enough to attend. She was eight years old. Camp started on Sunday afternoon. We arrived as soon as the gates opened because she couldn't wait to get started!

Notes:

Notes:

On Monday, I received a phone call from the Camp Director. He said, "Joy, I'm sorry to call you; but, I think you'd better come pick her up. She's been sick all night. Several other campers have the same thing and we're taking care of them in the Infirmary." I told him I would be there right away. When I arrived, the Camp Director met me and walked with me to the Infirmary. He assured me that she seemed to be a little better. Then, he said, "I'm fairly sure that they all have some sort of stomach bug that won't last long; but I know that if she stays and doesn't feel well, she won't ever want to come back." I agreed with him. So, her first week at camp turned out to be less than one day long.

The story doesn't end there. After we left camp, the Camp Director took his camera up to The Falls and made a picture of the waterfalls and the swimming hole. He had it printed up and wrote a note on it for her, "I'll look forward to having you at Camp next summer!" She received it before the end of the week and even though she was only at camp one night, she had a good experience and something to look forward to. She wanted to go back and she wasn't afraid that the same thing would happen again. She returned as a camper the following summer and every summer after that, except one, until she graduated from high school. She worked as a counselor for the camp while she was in college, and now, she is a mentor for one of the current counselors.

My story illustrates operating procedures that are effective in carrying out the mission of the camp. Here are the procedures:

- Camper registration: all the necessary parental contact information and medical information for the camper was collected at registration, and was available to the staff members when she got sick.
- The counselor in her cabin took her, and the other sick campers, to the Infirmary as soon as the need arose. Another counselor in her cabin stayed with the campers who did not get sick. The camp was staffed according to established and prudent ratios of adults to children and thus, no campers were left alone.
- The Infirmary was staffed by a Camp Nurse who was experienced and able to care for the campers overnight, along with other staffers for assistance.
- The Camp Director contacted me and gave me infor-

mation as well as guidance for making the decision to come pick up my camper.

- The Camp Director made an effort to encourage my daughter, in spite of the first night's experience, to plan to come back again.

Let's think about how this camper's experience might have been different if the camp hadn't followed safe operating procedures. When she got sick, the Director wouldn't have known, because it wasn't given in the registration information that she was allergic to certain medications and foods. He might not have had complete contact information and thus would have been delayed in contacting her parents. If the Infirmary wasn't adequately staffed, then the campers and counselors would have had a much more difficult experience during the night. When the Director was slow to contact the camper's parents, the result might have been anger from the parents instead of understanding. In today's world, angry parents might have come to get their child and then looked for a way to assert a claim that the camp was negligent in its operations and its supervision of the children. Claims of negligence against church camps have actually been made in recent years. The results have included serious harm to the camps' reputations as well as financial losses.

Other operating procedures are also important for camping programs. Using facilities, cabins, or camp sites, that do not provide opportunities for adults to isolate one child in secret locations greatly reduces the likelihood of child abuse. First aid training for all staffers is a key to handing sports injuries, or insect bites, or other emergencies effectively. Having staff members experienced and trained in leadership of the camp activities, such as horseback riding, rock climbing, swimming, and hiking minimizes the risks of injuries and helps to assure good experiences for all. Training all staffers in appropriate reporting procedures when an accident, or incident of child abuse is reported, is certainly important. As a part of that training, it is recommended that staffers be trained to model appropriate interpersonal boundaries, self-respect, and respect for others, through their use of language, touch, nurture, and discipline. The American Camping Association (www.acacamps.org) has developed comprehensive guidelines for safely operating camps for children, youth, and adults. The General Board of Discipleship of the United Methodist Church (www.gbod.org) has extensive camping ministry resources available for use by congregations and larger groups.

Notes: _____

_____

_____

_____

_____

_____

_____

_____

_____

_____

_____

_____

Notes: _____

_____

_____

_____

_____

_____

_____

_____

_____

_____

_____

Adequate Insurance for the Scope of Your Ministries

Every local church must have adequate property and liability insurance for the scope of its ministry. *The Book of Discipline of the United Methodist Church* requires the trustees of each local church to secure adequate insurance. (see ¶ 2532.2.) In addition, your church should have insurance for workers compensation claims, motor vehicles, directors and officers, and employment practices. If your congregation is *never* involved in ministries that involve transporting people in motor vehicles, then perhaps it can afford not to carry insurance for such occasions. This is very unlikely, however, just as it is very unlikely that a local church will never be involved with children in any way. If your church has no ministry with children or youth it must be heavily involved with ministry to senior adults! No matter what ages your ministries include, your church cannot afford to do without adequate insurance.

Each local church that adopts a Safe Sanctuaries plan for the prevention of child abuse will be able to secure affordable insurance coverage.

Part Three: Youth

The Scope of the Problem

EVERY YEAR, our local churches provide confirmation studies for youth. At the worship service in which the youth are confirmed in my congregation, our pastor will address the entire congregation, saying, "Brothers and sisters, I commend to your love and care these persons whom we this day receive into the [professing] membership of this congregation. Do all in your power to increase their faith, confirm their hope, and perfect them in love." The congregation will respond with the following promise and covenant, "We rejoice to recognize you as [professing] members of Christ's holy church, and bid you welcome to this congregation of The United Methodist Church. With you we renew our vows to uphold it by our prayers, our presence, our gifts, our service, and our witness. With God's help we will so order our lives after the example of Christ that, surrounded by steadfast love, you may be established in the faith, and confirmed and strengthened in the way that leads to life eternal" ("Baptismal Covenant III," *The United Methodist Hymnal;* pages 48–49). Making this promise gives each and every person in the congregation a sacred role and responsibility in the lives of the newly confirmed youth.

How often have you stopped to think about what your sacred responsibility is for the youth in your congregation? How can your congregation flesh out that responsibility? All the members of our congregations understand that at the baptism or confirmation of youth and children we are not simply spectators but are true participants. By our pledge, we are committed to lead our lives in ways that demonstrate to the youth the ways of Christ and the highest standards of Christian discipleship. Therefore, we are called to assure that our churches are places where youth can experience fellowship and nurture without fear of being injured or abused. Unfortunately, we cannot accomplish our goal by simply throwing open the doors of the church building and proclaiming, "Let's have some fellowship!" Today, we must live out our responsibility by organizing our ministries with youth in ways that will protect them as they explore what for them are the new and abstract mysteries of Christian faith. Furthermore, we

Notes:

_____

_____

_____

_____

_____

_____

_____

_____

_____

_____

_____

_____

OUR EFFORTS TO PROTECT
the youth will also protect adults
who work with youth.

must organize our ministries in ways that will protect the adults who work with youth from unfounded and false allegations of abuse or inappropriate behavior. Without a strong cadre of adult leaders who feel trusted and valued by the church, youth ministry will come to a screeching halt.

Research has shown convincingly that an overwhelming majority of American teenagers believe in God. A recent poll conducted by Gallup found that 95% of teenagers believe in God, 42% pray alone frequently, 36% read Scriptures at least weekly, and 45% belong to a church-sponsored youth group and attend worship services weekly. The same research indicates that youth practicing their faith are individuals who possess a greater measure of positive values and demonstrate more caring behaviors than age-group peers who lack involvement with religious groups. Approximately 75% of teens are members of religious groups. Within these groups, 62% of the members do volunteer service work and 56% make charitable contributions. These facts are mirrored in the findings of other research that show that church attendance and religious affiliation are positively associated with concern for the needy and willingness to help others. When we pay attention to findings such as these, we realize that the data substantiates what we intuitively know and feel about the importance of providing opportunities for our youth to actively participate in the community of faith. Opportunities for participation in youth ministry provide formative experiences that support teens as they explore and acquire values consistent with our Christian faith.

Another dimension needs to be considered: The teenager's affiliation with a community of faith is a source of strength to him or her for reducing high-risk behaviors, such as alcohol and drug use, antisocial behavior, premature and unsafe sexual behaviors, and suicide. This list of risky behaviors looks as if it could have come from the current generation of teens, or any generation in the recent past. Adults today can remember making choices about abusing illegal drugs and alcohol, about engaging in unsafe sexual behaviors, and even about suicide. However, adults know something else: Teens facing these challenges now are, in many cases, doing so with fewer resources to support them. This reality makes the availability of Safe Sanctuaries for youth ministry ever more crucial. The Gallup Organization, in the research mentioned, found that youth involved with congregations were more likely to choose abstinence from alcohol and drugs, more likely to abstain from unsafe sexual behaviors, and less likely to attempt suicide. The significance of this relationship is further illustrated by the Gallup research. The poll indicates that alcohol use and abuse was a problem in 30% of the teens' families. The National Center for Health Statistics has reported that suicide is the second leading cause of death among children and youth under twenty-one years of age. Additionally, it was estimated that for every completed suicide, there are fifty to one hundred attempted adolescent suicides. The National School Safety Center reports that crimes against children and youth at school include approximately 282,000 students who are physically attacked in our secondary schools each month.

In today's world, it would be nearly impossible for any of us not to hear about incidents of abuse and violence against youth. Most abusers are people known by the teen victims. The vast majority of abusers are adults on whom the victims are physically and emotionally dependent. As recently as 2000, three million incidents of abuse were reported in the United States. As shocking as that number is, those three million reported incidents actually involved nearly five million children and youth. Child advocacy experts estimate that six million more incidents go unreported each year. Such incidents happen all too frequently, with each day bringing new horrors to light. Although abuse and violence against youth has existed in Atlanta (where I live) and probably in every community for a long time, I have observed several trends that are fairly recent developments. First, there is considerably more news coverage of such abuse and incidents of violence. Second, there is more frequent and more effective prosecution, at local, state, and federal levels, of crimes against children and youth. Third, there are almost daily reports of abuse and violence perpetrated against youth in churches by people known, trusted, and respected by the victims. Fourth, victims of such abuse in churches, and their families and advocates, are more and more willing to seek redress through cooperating with criminal prosecutions or pursuing litigation against the perpetrators and the churches.

News coverage of abuse against youth in the recent past has included stories of priests and other clergy abusing teens in their churches, a youth director abusing a teenager on the bus used for youth group transportation, a recreation director molesting adolescent participants in the church's sports program, and a church camp counselor sexually abusing a camper. This list is not exhaustive; it is merely illustrative of the undeniable fact that we must work harder than ever

Notes: _____

_____

_____

_____

_____

_____

_____

_____

_____

_____

_____

_____

YOUTH MINISTRY IN SAFE sanctuaries not only reduces the risk of abuse but will also equip the youth with the faith and hope they need to face the present and the future.

Notes:
_____
_____
_____
_____
_____
_____
_____
_____
_____
_____
_____
_____
_____

WHAT IS ABUSE?

Abuse may include

–Physical abuse

–Emotional abuse

–Neglect

–Sexual Abuse

–Ritual Abuse

before to protect the youth in our care, recognizing that whatever efforts we have made up to this day have been only a beginning. We must also recognize that our efforts to protect the youth will protect adults who work with youth as well.

Most congregations I am familiar with do well at providing ministries for the youth that will increase their faith, such as Sunday school, Bible study, confirmation studies, and other educational settings. Most congregations also do well at providing ministries for developing a strong commitment to service among the youth through special projects, fellowship opportunities, mission trips, retreats, and other such settings. What about confirming their hope? How does your congregation address this facet of its responsibility for youth? In just a few short sentences, we have demonstrated that today's world is frequently an unfriendly and dangerous place for teens. Youth face the possibility of violence and abuse at home, at school, on the street, and everywhere else. Nevertheless, the youth who are connected to a community of faith seem to have greater strength with which to face these difficult circumstances. They seem to have more coping skills and a larger measure of optimism that today's hardships are not the end. In other words, they are more hopeful that today's situation, whether it is parental abuse, random violence, or anything else, is temporary and the future will be healthful and good. I believe the explanation for this is that the youth involved with a community of faith have been blessed by their interactions with, and relationships to, a number of nurturing, caring, compassionate adult leaders who over time are modeling a Christian approach to daily life. In light of the facts and statistics cited here, as well as the constant stream of media reports, we can conclude that providing youth ministries in Safe Sanctuaries not only reduces the risk of abuse within the church but will also equip the youth with the faith and hope they need to face the present and the future.

The full spectrum of the problem of abuse and violence against youth is far too broad to be comprehensively addressed here. For our purposes, we must limit our focus to the prevention of abuse in the church and its ministries. Acknowledging our limited focus does not mean there is not a lot to consider. The gospel message clearly calls our communities of faith to engage in ministries with youth that are nurturing, sustaining, and compassionate. Our society needs our communities of faith to surround youth with steadfast love so that they can be strong in the face of difficult challenges and choices. Planning for Safe Sanctuaries in youth ministries requires us to focus on at least three groups: youth, workers with youth, and the church as a whole congregation. Planning for youth includes planning for junior highs, middle highs, and senior highs. Planning for the workers with youth includes planning for pastors, youth ministers and directors, youth Sunday school teachers, youth group counselors, youth music workers, camp directors and staff members, retreat leaders, and even those who substitute when the regular workers cannot be present. Planning for the congregation includes planning for the board of trustees, the staff-parish committee, and many others.

Types of Abuse Against Youth

Generally, abuse is categorized in five primary forms: physical abuse, emotional abuse, neglect, sexual abuse, and ritual abuse. The resolution passed by General Conference calls all congregations to work to prevent all of these forms of abuse. Although we may typically think of young children when we think of these forms of abuse, youth can be victims of each and every one of these abuses.

1. **Physical Abuse**
   This is abuse in which a person deliberately and intentionally causes bodily harm to a youth or young child. Examples may include violent battery with a weapon (such as a knife or belt), burning, choking, fracturing bones, and other nonaccidental injuries.

2. **Emotional Abuse**
   This is abuse in which a person exposes a youth or younger child to spoken and/or unspoken violence or emotional cruelty. Emotional abuse sends a message to the youth that he or she is worthless, bad, unloved, and undeserving of love and care. Youth exposed to emotional abuse may have experienced being deprived of all parental affection, being locked in closets or other confining spaces, being incessantly told they are bad, or being forced to abuse alcohol or illegal drugs. This type of abuse is difficult to prove and is devastating to the victim.

3. **Neglect**
   This is abuse in which a person endangers a youth's health, welfare, and safety through negligence. It may include withholding food, medical care, affection, and even education to destroy the youth's sense of self-esteem and self-worth. Neglect may well be the most common form of abuse. Although it is often difficult to prove, reports of neglect from teenagers should not be ignored.

Notes: _____

_____

_____

_____

_____

_____

_____

_____

_____

_____

_____

_____

THE YOUTH VICTIM IS NEVER responsible for causing the abuse and should never be blamed for it.

Notes: _____

_____

_____

_____

_____

_____

_____

_____

_____

_____

_____

_____

No Church is Immune
from the horrors of abuse
simply because it wants to be.

4. Sexual Abuse

This type of abuse occurs when sexual contact between a youth and an adult (or older, more powerful youth) happens. The youth victim is not capable of consenting to such contact or resisting such sexual acts. Often, the youth victim is physically dependent on the perpetrator (for example, a parent). Additionally, the youth victim is often psychologically dependent on the perpetrator (for example, a teacher or a youth minister). Examples of sexual abuse include fondling, intercourse, incest, and the exploitation of and exposure to pornography and/or prostitution.

5. Ritual Abuse

This is abuse in which physical, sexual, or psychological violence is inflicted on a youth, intentionally and in a stylized way, by someone (or multiple persons) with responsibility for the victim's welfare. Typically, the perpetrator appeals to some higher authority or power to justify his or her abuses. Examples of ritual abuse may include cruel treatment of animals or repetitious threats of sexual or physical violence to the youth victim or to people related to the youth victim. When reports of ritual abuse are made, they are often extremely horrifying. Such reports may even seem too gruesome to be true. Never ignore a youth who makes a report of this type of abuse.

It Can Happen Anywhere

When a youth reports that he or she has experienced the behaviors detailed in these descriptions, serious attention should be paid to the report. While not every teenager's story is actually a report of abuse, the truth needs to be determined to prevent both further harm to the youth or further false allegations.

Abuse of a youth or child is criminal behavior and is punished severely in every state. Although each state has its own specific legal definition, sexual abuse exploits and harms youth by involving them in sexual behavior for which they are unprepared, to which they cannot consent, and from which they are unable to protect themselves.

The youth victim is never responsible for causing the abuse and should never be blamed for it. The youth victim is not capable of consent to abusive behavior, either legally or morally. Sexual abuse of youth is always wrong and is solely the responsibility of the abuser. In some instances, the abuser who is confronted will respond defensively, saying things like, "What abuse? She wanted it!" or "What abuse? He needed some love, and I provided it." Responses such as these must not distract us from the fact that the victim was quite likely dependent on the abuser in some way and unable to defend him- or herself against the acts of the abuser. For example, the victim is a student who is afraid that rejecting the teacher or coach will lead to repercussions in class or on the team. Another unfortunate but not uncommon scenario is a youth who is singled out by a youth minister or counselor for special attention. In the event the abuse is reported, the abuser's initial response may be something like, "I would never abuse one of my youth. She was having a rough time at home, and I was just trying to help." Another common response is, "He needed a loving relationship to learn about God's love, and I helped show him God's will." Needless to say, abuse of youth is never a reflection of or an incarnation of God's will in the Christian faith. Furthermore, such a claim is not, and should not be, a successful defense to an accusation of abuse.

The church must work to assure youth and families that abuse will not be tolerated or ignored in the community of faith. The church can demonstrate its commitment to providing a safe, secure place where all youth can grow in faith and wisdom by seriously addressing the need to develop and implement abuse prevention policies and strategies for every congregation.

Frequently, when congregations are first considering the task of developing a youth abuse prevention policy and strategy, one or more members may respond, "Well, this is silly. Such a horrible thing would never happen in our church!" Or, "I think we're blowing this issue out of proportion. Just because it happens in the big city churches doesn't mean it would ever happen here." Or, "We never have as many volunteer leaders for Sunday school and UMYF as we need. If we start making each worker answer a lot of questions and sign a covenant, we will scare everybody off. Then what will we do?" Or, "I don't see much point in this, since the youth don't come to the church often, anyway."

Comments such as these demonstrate not only our reluctance to admit that tragedies of abuse are real for many teenagers but also our complete abhorrence of the thought that such crimes could happen in our churches. Perhaps comments of this nature reveal our unfailing optimism that atrocities cannot happen in *our* church.

Knowing the Facts

When abuse occurs in our own neighborhoods, it gets our attention and sometimes serves as a catalyst in a way that

Notes: _____

_____

_____

_____

_____

_____

_____

_____

_____

_____

_____

_____

Notes: _____

_____

_____

_____

_____

_____

_____

_____

_____

_____

_____

_____

The Concept of Charitable

immunity, which in the past shielded churches from many types of litigation, no longer serves as a viable protection in cases of abuse or sexual misconduct.

nameless and faceless teenagers counted in statistics cannot. However, it is important to know a few statistics:

- Childhelp USA, (www.childhelp.org) one of the largest and oldest nonprofit organizations dedicated to the treatment and prevention of child abuse, reports that in 2000 approximately three million incidents of child abuse and neglect to child protective service agencies in the United States. This number represents children and youth through the age of eighteen. (These statistics were compiled from the U.S. Department of Health and Human Services, Children's Bureau.)
- Studies have estimated that one out of three girls is sexually abused before the age of eighteen. Similarly, one out of seven boys has been sexually abused before the age of eighteen. Even more frightening is that these numbers may be underestimated, since many youth are reluctant to report abuse.
- Childhelp USA also reports that approximately 1,200 deaths attributable to child abuse and/or neglect occur each year. This number includes deaths of youth attributed to physical abuse, sexual abuse, neglect, and emotional abuse; however, most of the children who die are under the age of six. That number of deaths equates to more than three children and youth dying each day.

Let's think again about the first number listed: 3,000,000 incidents of abuse per year. That equals 8,219 youth or children abused each day; 342 abused per hour; nearly 6 (5.7) abused every minute; and one abused every 10 seconds of every hour of every day, including the sabbath.

The Church at Risk

In light of statistics such as these, it seems that any church involved with youth is a place where abuse could occur. What makes the risk for churches especially high? The following factors can be named:

- Churches generally act as organizations with a high level of trust in their members, relying on the members and leaders to conduct themselves following the example of Christ. Sometimes this trusting attitude persists even in the face of questions or reports of misconduct.
- Churches are famously passive, and even inactive, when it comes to screening the volunteers and/or employees who work with youth. Often, no investigation is done at all before total strangers are welcomed aboard as new volunteer leaders.
- Churches routinely provide opportunities for close contact and close personal relationships with youth. Such

relationships are sometimes encouraged without giving the workers sufficient education and training on establishing and maintaining healthy and appropriate interpersonal boundaries with the youth.

Simultaneously with the growth of the church's need for greater numbers of workers with youth, there has been an explosion in litigation against the church for incidents of sexual abuse of youth and for claims of clergy sexual misconduct. Every state now has strong statutory requirements in place for the reporting of an incident of abuse. This, coupled with the unrelenting attention focused by the media on the teenage victims and the church, has increased the number of criminal charges against the accused perpetrators of abuse as well as the number of civil lawsuits seeking monetary damages for the injuries suffered by the young victims. These civil lawsuits often name multiple defendants, including the accused perpetrator, the local church where the accused perpetrator was an employee or volunteer, and the annual conference. In lawsuits such as these, the victim (plaintiff) generally claims that one individual sexually abused him or her and that the church and/or the annual conference was negligent in hiring and supervising the individual abuser, thus increasing the possibility that the youth would be injured.

The concept of charitable immunity, which in the past shielded churches from many types of litigation, no longer serves as a viable protection in cases of abuse or sexual misconduct. In the past, our society afforded immunity from lawsuits to organizations such as churches that were seen to be providing charitable services to the community. In other words, the churches were protected from lawsuits because their value to society as a whole was seen to be more important that any individual's possible claims of injury. Today, the public and the courts consider the harm done by abuse of youth or children too great to allow such incidents to go unreported and unpunished. Frequently, the punishment comes in the form of monetary damages in huge verdicts against the perpetrator and/or the institution in which the perpetrator worked or volunteered. These damage awards range from thousands to many millions of dollars. Often, the trial jury awards an amount far exceeding the value of the church's insurance coverage, leaving the church in danger of not being able to continue in ministry. While a church cannot guarantee the safety of every person within its community and ministries, every church can be responsible for reducing and eliminating circumstances that could lead to harm or injury.

Notes:

_____

_____

_____

_____

_____

_____

_____

_____

_____

_____

_____

_____

_____

Teens Suffering Abuse

often do not tell anyone about it; therefore, it is important to recognize other signs of abuse.

Notes: _____

_____

_____

_____

_____

_____

_____

_____

_____

_____

_____

_____

Recognizing and understanding the frequency of the occurrence of abuse of youth and children is only part of the task. In each local congregation, we must know how to recognize indicators of possible abuse and learn ways to safely carry out our ministries without unnecessarily or unwittingly providing opportunities for abusers to harm youth. In addition, we must understand the requirements of state laws for reporting suspected incidents of abuse and develop a plan for following these requirements when the need arises.

The church must not look upon the reality of abuse of youth as a reason to withdraw from its ministries with youth. More than ever before, the youth in our communities need strong leadership from Christian role models to equip them with spiritual strength to face everyday challenges in school, at work, and in social arenas. We must work to assure that our ministries are carried out in responsibly safe circumstances. We, as members of the community of faith, are called to remember the pledge we have made as each youth is confirmed. Remembering that, we are called to make the church a safe and holy place where youth will be strengthened in their faith and nurtured into healthy young adults.

Indicators of Youth Abuse

Teens suffering abuse often do not tell anyone about it; therefore, it is important to be able to recognize other signs of abuse. The following characteristics may be indicators of abuse, although they are not necessarily proof. Individually, any one of the indicators may be a sign of a number of other more or less serious problems. When these indicators are observed in a youth, they can be considered as warnings and lead you to look into the situation further.

Possible Signs of Physical Abuse
1. Hostile and aggressive behavior toward others;
2. Fearfulness of parents and/or other adults;
3. Destructive behavior toward self, others, and/or property;
4. Burns, facial injuries, pattern of repetitious bruises.

Possible Signs of Emotional Abuse
1. Severe depression and/or withdrawal;
2. Severe lack of self-esteem;
3. Threatening or attempting suicide;
4. Eating and/or speech disorders;
5. Going to extremes to seek adult approval;
6. Extreme passive/aggressive behavior patterns.

Possible Signs of Neglect
1. Pattern of inappropriate dress for climate;
2. Begging or stealing food/chronic hunger;
3. Depression;
4. Untreated medical conditions;
5. Poor hygiene.

Possible Signs of Sexual Abuse
1. Unusually advanced sexual knowledge and/or behavior for teen's age and developmental stage;
2. Depression—cries often for no apparent reason;
3. Promiscuous behavior;
4. Running away from home and refusing to return;
5. Difficulty walking or sitting;
6. Bruises/bleeding in vaginal or anal areas;
7. Frequent headaches, stomachaches, extreme fatigue;
8. Sexually transmitted diseases.

In addition to these indicators, youth who have been sexually abused at church may exhibit some of the following:
1. Unusual nervousness or anxiety about going to the Sunday school class alone;
2. Reluctance to participate in church activities that were previously enthusiastically approached;
3. Comments such as "I don't want to be alone with _____," in reference to a Sunday school teacher or youth group counselor;
4. Nightmares involving a youth group adult leader or a Sunday school teacher as a frightening character;
5. Unexplained hostility toward a youth group adult leader or teacher.

Possible Signs of Ritual Abuse
1. Disruptions of memory or consciousness;
2. Unexplained mistrust and mood swings;
3. Flashbacks;
4. Eating disorders;
5. Fear of the dark, especially at sundown or a full moon;
6. Agitation, anxiety, or despair that seems to occur in cycles;
7. Fear of ministers, priests, or others wearing robes or uniforms;
8. Nightmares or sleep disorders;
9. Any of the symptoms of sexual abuse.

Abuse of youth and children occurs every minute of every day, in every community. Such abuse occurs in every economic, racial, ethnic, religious, or other demographic group.

Notes: _____
_____
_____
_____
_____
_____
_____
_____
_____
_____
_____
_____
_____

WHO ARE ABUSERS?
Abusers are not easily recognizable, for they may look just like you or me. Abusers are people who have greater power in relation to a youth, and they use that power to harm the youth.

Notes: _____

_____

_____

_____

_____

_____

_____

_____

_____

_____

_____

_____

WITHOUT A COMPREHENSIVE strategy against abuse, we are taking a needless risk that harm may be done to our youth and our workers with youth.

No segment of our society is immune or untouched. As Christians, we are called to be vigilant in protecting the youth in our midst and in preventing abuse in the community of faith. For many congregations, this will seem to be an impossible task. However, there are certain specific actions that can be easily taken, and with appropriate planning they will enable the congregation to move forward in providing Safe Sanctuaries for its youth ministries. These plans and actions are detailed in the following chapters.

Abusers: Who Are They?

To prevent the abuse of youth in our churches, we must not only recognize the signs of abuse but also realize that the abusers of our youth are more often than not familiar adults who are trusted by the youth. Less than twenty percent of abuse of youth is perpetrated by strangers. In other words, in more than three quarters of the reported incidents of abuse, the victim is related to or acquainted with the abuser.

Youth victims of sexual abuse and the people who abuse them come from all segments of our society. Abusers can be found in every racial, ethnic, economic, and social group. They look much like us. Abusers can be charismatic leaders, especially those who work or volunteer with youth. They are sociable and willing to include the youth in their adult social events, and some are sympathetic to troubled teens. Some are married and have children, and some are unmarried; some are young, and some are older adults. Within my community in recent years, abusers have been identified as a youth detention center chaplain, foster parents, teachers, coaches, a church recreation ministry director, youth ministers, and pastors. In other words, the variety is unlimited.

Who are the abusers within our churches? They may be Sunday school teachers, camp counselors, youth group counselors, clergy, another youth or child, or anyone else with unlimited and unsupervised access to youth.

How Does Abuse Happen?

Sexual abuse of youth happens when a person exerts his or her power over a youth in ways that harm and/or exploit the youth. Another way of thinking about it is that the abuser is powerful because he or she has many more resources than the victim, and the youth is vulnerable perhaps in several ways. The abuser gains power over the youth victim using multiple sources: size, position, knowledge, money, just to name a few. All of these things work to make the abuser believe that he or she is able to behave abusively toward a youth and that the victim will be unable to repel or stop the abusive behavior. If the victim is physically smaller and weaker, intellectually less mature, and economically dependent on the abuser for sustenance, the abuser can readily take advantage of those circumstances. When a teen's vulnerability and an abuser's misuse of power combine with the opportunity to exploit the teen without being discovered, sexual abuse may, and often does, occur. Ministries planned and designed to minimize the possibilities of isolation of individual teens and opportunities for adult leaders to demand secrecy will provide greater protection for the youth and the workers.

Members of our churches do not like to think that any person in the Sunday school or any other ministry of the church would harm any of the youth. Conversely, we do not like to think that false allegations of abuse could be made by any youth in the church. But without a comprehensive strategy against abuse, we are taking a needless risk that harm may be done to our youth and our workers with youth.

It is imperative for our churches not to adopt or implement abuse prevention policies that apply to only a few categories of people. Strategies must be supported by the whole congregation and carried out by applying the same policies and requirements to each worker involved in youth ministries, including the clergy. When a congregation adopts an abuse prevention strategy that applies only to the paid youth workers or only to professional staff members, it is doomed to be no more than partially successful. It exempts too many people from the strategy's requirements and may create specific opportunities for abusers to have unlimited access to youth.

Consequences of Sexual Abuse of Youth

When one youth is sexually abused within our church, many victims are created, including the youth, the youth's family, the congregation, and the family of the abuser. For example, if the youth minister sexually abuses a girl in the middle-high youth group and the girl reports the abuse, she may be physically injured and traumatized. She may also be doubted by others who do not want to believe such a thing could have happened. Her family will be outraged, frightened, and possibly doubted by others in the faith community. The congregation itself will likely divide into factions comprised of those who believe the youth and those who believe the accused abuser. Such divisions have been known to last for years. Finally, the abuser's family may suffer devastating

Notes: _____

_____

_____

_____

_____

_____

_____

_____

_____

_____

_____

_____

_____

ABUSE IN THE CHURCH

creates many victims:

−the youth

−the youth's family

−the congregation

−the family of the abuser

Notes: _____

_____

_____

_____

_____

_____

_____

_____

_____

_____

_____

The Congregation May

suffer for a long time when civil or criminal litigation ensues as a result of the abuse.

consequences as a result of the loss of income and the possibility that the abuser will be sentenced to prison.

Of foremost importance is the youth who has been harmed; he or she must be cared for. Innocence has been stolen from the victim. The trauma of abuse may cause emotional injury as well as physical injury, and these scars will last through the victim's life. When sexual abuse is perpetrated by a trusted person in the church, even greater harm is done to the teen's faith in God and faith in the church. The victim may struggle with questions: If God loves everyone, how could God have let this happen to me? How can the members of this congregation continue praying and singing week after week, acting as if nothing has happened? For youth, this is a common and strong reaction. Experiences of abuse in the church create massive obstacles to a teen victim's development of a living, sustaining faith. Since this abuse occurs at the time when the youth is likely to be exploring the importance of making a lifetime faith commitment, this abuse can destroy the youth's desire to participate in the community of faith. This consequence is no less important than the physical injuries or the eventual depression, fear, and lack of sufficient self-esteem that often develop as a result of sexual abuse. For the individual victim and for the community of faith, this result is devastating.

The congregation also becomes a victim after abuse is revealed. Members are stunned that such a crime could have been perpetrated within their midst and are humiliated at their failure to maintain the church as a safe sanctuary for youth. Members fear that they are ill equipped to help the teen's healing process. They are angry that a person welcomed into their fellowship would dare to disregard the gospel's mandate by abusing any of the youth. Often, members are divided when the congregation begins to think about how to address all of the problems created by the incident. They agonize over how to develop strategies for safety and how to provide the ministries of healing and nurture to the victim and the victim's family.

In addition, the congregation may suffer for a long time when civil or criminal litigation ensues as a result of the abuse. Litigation in the courts can keep the incident alive for months, even years, and may make resolution of the emotional issues even more difficult. Within the past three years, we have seen daily news reports of the consequences and costs of civil and criminal litigation involving churches and clergy-persons accused of sexual abuses. A growing trend toward criminal prosecution of abusers can be observed in the cases being reported. When convictions result, the sentences often range from ten years to life in prison for the defendant. However, we cannot yet say that the trend toward criminal prosecutions is reducing the number of civil lawsuits being pursued against churches for claims of negligent hiring, retention, or supervision. These criminal prosecutions and civil suits, along with possible bankruptcy proceedings, will quite possibly consume the resources of churches for the foreseeable future. In the meantime, the congregations will suffer as resources for ministry decline and confidence in leadership erodes. Ultimately, such a situation may lead not only to financial bankruptcy but also to a spiritual bankruptcy that would be even more difficult to recover from than financial ruin. As a result of many reports and situations like these, we have finally become aware of the effects of the long, time-consuming, and costly litigation process on congregations and denominational organizations.

Although criminal or civil litigation is often necessary in such situations, the litigation process itself will not provide what is needed for healing among the congregation's members. For this healing, the community of faith must dig deeply into its biblical foundations and find strength to conquer the evils of fear and the lack of knowledge about abuse. The congregation must make a renewed commitment to living out the gospel's call to provide continuing opportunities for the youth to grow in faith.

Finally, the financial consequences of sexual abuse in the church cannot be ignored. As reports of abuse and lawsuits increase, the financial costs rise exponentially. A victim of sexual abuse and his or her family will suffer financially, since the costs of counseling and medical treatment go up each year. A congregation need only ask its insurance agent for the latest statistics to learn that the amounts paid by churches, as settlements or verdicts in abuse cases, can be astronomical—ranging from thousands to millions of dollars.

No congregation can afford—financially, ethically, or morally—to fail to implement strategies for the reduction and prevention of sexual abuse of its youth. We, as Christians, are not called to discontinue our congregations' ministries with children and youth. We are called to engage in these ministries with enthusiasm and with the knowledge that we are making every effort to provide ministry to our youth in ways that assure their safety while they grow in sustaining faith.

Notes: _____

_____

_____

_____

_____

_____

_____

_____

_____

_____

_____

_____

Basic Procedures for Safe Ministry With Youth

chapter six

THESE SAFE SANCTUARIES procedures are designed to make youth ministry flow smoothly by reducing the possibility of harm to the youth and to the workers with youth. Each of the following procedures is important in the congregation's comprehensive Safe Sanctuaries strategy.

Appropriate Interpersonal Boundaries

Youth ministry can be described by many adjectives, but the first one is almost always *relational*. Youth get involved, and stay involved, with youth ministries because the ministries offer opportunities to experience relationships with peers and adults that are healthy, both physically and spiritually. Whether they can articulate this or not, the youth want and need to see good examples from the adult leaders of appropriate ways to relate to others. Adults who model respectful and nurturing behaviors that do not interfere with another's privacy provide these types of good examples. The youth will follow the lead of the adults in this regard; therefore, it is important for the adult workers to be clear about appropriate behaviors. Adult workers must be attentive to appropriate dress codes (some groups have found it effective to adopt actual dress codes for retreats, trips, and regular meetings), appropriate use of language, and appropriate demonstrations of affection and encouragement. A good rule of thumb for adult leaders is to never initiate a hug and to always be the one to end the hug. A retired junior high and high school educator put it this way, "If it's not yours, don't touch it." In other words, offer hugs when they are requested, but do not ever impose your touches on the youth in your group. Whenever a question arises about where to draw appropriate interpersonal boundaries, remember that you are the adult and it is your responsibility to behave professionally, even if you are a volunteer.

73

Notes: _____

_____

_____

_____

_____

_____

_____

_____

_____

_____

_____

BEFORE GOING ON A TRIP,

both the youth and the adult leaders must think through the needs for a simple and respectful code of conduct.

Safe Sanctuaries and Cyber Safety for Ministries with Children and Youth

Today's world is a markedly different place for our children, youth, and families than the world we knew fifteen years ago. When we survey the variety of ways we have to communicate with each other, it is clear that dramatic changes have occurred and are continuing to influence the ways we live, and work, and engage in ministry. In October 2007, the General Board of Discipleship of the United Methodist Church sponsored a conference focused on cyber safety in ministry with children and youth. The conference explored the many ways that technology is used for communication in our ministries. More important, the participants learned ways to use communication technologies safely and helpfully in ministries with children, youth, and families. At the conclusion of the conference, the participants agreed on the following points:

1. Children and youth are more skilled today than ever before at using a number of different technologies for communication and learning.
2. Children and youth are more comfortable using communication technologies than their parents, teachers, and ministers.
3. In today's youth culture, there is a generally recognized pattern of communicating through technology that indicates the level of knowledge the communicators have about each other.
4. Parents, teachers, ministers, and other leaders are trying to understand communication technology as well as the youth; and they are concerned that they do not know enough to be able to use the technology safely and teach others to use it safely.
5. Ministers, teachers, parents, and other adult leaders know that using technology such email, cell phones, text messages, and the internet has become commonplace in ministry and acknowledge that we must master it—we can't go forward without gaining new knowledge and skills for ministry.

The General Conference of the United Methodist Church, in 1988, passed a resolution condemning the exploitation of women and children in pornography, including print and video media. Frankly, at that time, it might have been hard for most local church youth ministers to imagine that youth were routinely being harassed and abused by being exploited for pornographic productions. That is no longer so hard to imagine. Instead, the truth of such exploitation and abuse cannot be denied or ignored. In the past twenty years, the need to understand the risks and benefits of using the internet and all the other new communication tools in education has exploded, especially for adults involved with children and youth. Every day we hear of new incidents of persons being hurt as a result of unscrupulous use of these new technologies and too often, the victims are children or teenagers. The more incidents we hear of, the more worried we become about the safety of our children and the members of our youth groups. Every day we are bombarded by advertising for new video games and game equipment, new music technology, and new radio and telephone technology.

Think about the first time you acquired a cordless phone. Remember what it looked like—a piece of equipment about the size of a quart of milk and about as heavy! Not too long after you got that cordless phone, you acquired a car phone. This was a phone that was installed in your car—it was a mobile phone because it went where your car went—but it only performed the functions that your phone at home performed. Today, only a few years after you installed that car phone, you may have given up on it and replaced it with a cell phone that performs the functions of a telephone, a camera, a video camera, a computer, a walkie-talkie, a calculator, and a global positioning system in a package smaller than a deck of cards! And, even more likely, you weren't able to utilize all the features of your newest cell phone without asking for instructions and explanations, and demonstrations, from your teenage son or daughter! Congratulations, you have become, as I have, what is kindly referred to as a cyber-immigrant—an adult who has come haltingly, hesitantly, and fearfully to the routine utilization of at least three communication technologies. While we have come to this at a snail's pace, our children have faced the new learning with much less trepidation and as a result, they are making more frequent use of the technologies with each passing day. They are proudly known as cyber-natives.

The Pew Internet and American Life Project , supported by The Pew Charitable Trusts as an initiative of the Pew Research Center, produces reports exploring the impact of the internet on families, communities, work and home, daily life, education, health care, and civic and political life. Some of the most recent reports contain information pertinent for those of us working to build Safe Sanctuaries in our ministries. You can find these reports at **www.pewinternet.org**. Here are some of the data reported: the surveys show that 73% of the adult respondents are users of the internet. Of those adults, 83% use the internet to seek information about

Notes:

_____

_____

_____

_____

_____

_____

_____

_____

_____

_____

_____

_____

STAFF MEMBERS IN A CAMP
setting should know how to respond to a request from a camper for a private conversation.

Notes:

_____

_____

_____

_____

_____

_____

_____

_____

_____

_____

_____

_____

A Church will Drastically
reduce the possibility of an incident of abuse by following the two-adult rule.

their hobbies, 57% of use the internet to watch and/or download video, and 87% of adults between the ages of eighteen and twenty-nine use the internet.

Our youth use the internet and other technologies to learn as well as to communicate and they also create content for the internet. According to the Pew reports, 64% of online teenagers between the ages of twelve and seventeen are creating content. One of the most prominent uses of the content the youth create is postings on social networking sites.

A social networking site is an online place were a user can set up a personal profile and then use it to set up a personal network of connections to other users of the site. Two of the most well known social networking sites are MySpace.com and Facebook.com but there are plenty of others. You can go online to www.toptenreviews.com to find information about the most frequently visited social networking sites. These types of online sites have been in the headlines frequently in stories of cyber stalking, cyber bullying, and sexual misconduct or abuse. However, according to the Pew reports, 55% of teens online use these types of sites, especially older teen girls. Teen girls who use these social networking sites use them mostly to reinforce the already existing friendships they have. Teen boys use the sites for making new contacts and friends. According to the Pew reports, more than half of all the online youth, ages 12–17, in the Unites States use social networking sites. (www.pewinternet.org). It seems obvious that if more than half of all teens online are using any type of website, for example the social networking sites, then leaders of youth ministry must become knowledgeable about such sites and how to use them safely for ministry purposes.

Not all internet sites are created equal in terms of appropriateness for use by children and youth. Learning to distinguish between sites that can be safely used and those that must be avoided is crucial for the developing communication skills of youth; therefore, it is also crucial for those of us leading ministry with youth and children. Furthermore, learning so that we can teach the parents of youth is crucial because we know that parents look to us for guidance almost as much as the youth do! Beyond these fundamentals, we, as leaders in ministry with children and youth, must also learn how to use the super communication technology available to us for the purposes of teaching the basic principles of the Christian faith. The leaders in every generation have been called to communicate meaningfully with the youth and we are no different. If teachers of math, science, history, and language can master the technology, then teachers of our faith can too!

The first, and probably most difficult, step to becoming knowledgeable in the appropriate uses of technology for ministry is to become knowledgeable about how easily technology can be abused to harm our children. To be successful at this, we must overcome our tendency to deny that our children and youth are at risk. None of us wants to think, much less believe that the safety of our children and teens is at risk whenever they go online. We think, "Yes, we've heard there are sexually explicit websites; but, our sons and daughters would never go to any of them." We think, "Yes, we've heard that sexual predators use the internet to search for victims; but, our children can't be found on the internet because they are good kids." To put it plainly, we think and act like the classic "Yes, buts" who always say, "Yes, child abuse might happen somewhere; but, it would never happen here."

Even I came late to belief in the dangers waiting for our children and youth online. It has taken me four or five years and meeting dozens of parents, teachers, ministers, and youth who have been harmed to fully realize that online dangers are real and that we can teach ourselves and our youth to use technology in ways that will reduce the risks of those online dangers. The end of my "Yes, but" attitude began with a phone call.

One summer day I received a call from a youth minister whom I have known and respected for a long time. When I answered the phone, I heard him say, "Joy, how soon can you come to do a Safe Sanctuaries training event for our staff?" I could hear a real urgency in his voice and I replied, "Well, how soon would you like? Would you like to have it before school starts, or early this fall?" The youth minister blurted out, "I was wondering if you could do it before the former youth director from the church down the street gets out of jail!"

Here is the rest of the story. The youth director who was in jail had seemed, before his incarceration, to be a dedicated worker. He had a good reputation among the parents and the congregation. He was technology savvy and I imagine he was proud of that. He was always one of the first to own the latest gadgets and techno-toys. It was no surprise when he traded in his first generation cell phone for a model that was equipped with a video camera. He began to use his cell phone camera to snap photos of the girls in the youth group

Notes:

_____

_____

_____

_____

_____

_____

_____

_____

_____

_____

_____

_____

Notes: _____

_____

_____

_____

_____

_____

_____

_____

_____

_____

_____

and then transfer the photos from the phone to his computer. The youth director made so many photos that the girls became extremely annoyed. They asked him to stop. He didn't. They insisted that he stop. He didn't. They complained to their parents. He still didn't stop. Then, the parents complained to the senior minister and an investigation resulted. The youth director's office computer was full of the photos and the investigation revealed that he had probably been downloading the photos to websites that the girls wouldn't have wanted to have their pictures. I learned from this how easily technology can be used for wrong, unacceptable, and harmful purposes.

On another day I got another phone call from a senior pastor. She said, "Joy, I would like to tell you a story and then ask you a question." Here is her story. On a Monday morning all the computers in the church's office network crashed. The senior pastor was the staff person who had set up the network and the one with the most computer knowledge, or so she thought. She told the youth director, the choir director, and the secretary to take the rest of the day off and she would try to recover the computers. She began by "rebooting" each computer individually. When she began to work on the youth director's computer, she found something she had not expected.

The computer's hard drive was completely filled, even overloaded, with pornography that had been downloaded from the internet. She called the youth director to come to the church. When he arrived, she confronted him about the content she found on the computer at his desk. He admitted that he had indeed downloaded the pornography and that he did it often. The senior pastor immediately terminated the youth director's employment at the church and escorted him from the property with instructions not to return. She actually had two questions for me. First, she asked if she did the right thing by terminating his employment. Second, she asked me if I had ever heard of such a thing before. My answer to both questions was, "Yes."

After several calls like these, I thought I had heard everything and there were no more surprises. I was wrong, but the surprise didn't come in a phone call. This time, it came in a conference when a fellow participant asked if he could tell me about an incident in his town. I listened to the following account.

A middle school student was invited by a friend to go with the youth group from the friend's church to spend the day at a local laser tag park. The group numbered in the dozens and a good number of adult leaders went along too. The park was busy that day with lots of kids and adults playing laser tag and other games. There were restroom and concession facilities at several locations in the park. Even though the adults who were accompanying the church youth group were attentive, they couldn't be everywhere and see all the youth at every minute.

At some point, the middle school student broke away from his group to go to the restroom. The others played on, knowing that he would catch up with them. But he didn't catch up. When he went into the restroom, he was followed by an adult man who, it was later learned, had been following him and waiting for an opportunity to separate him from the group. The man grabbed the student and forced him to leave the park with him. The student was threatened with physical harm if he didn't cooperate.

Outside the park, the man took the student with him to what appeared to be an empty warehouse nearby. However, the building was not empty. It was equipped as a movie and video production facility and a production session was in progress. The student was forced to give up his clothes and then was sexually abused as part of the filming of a pornographic video. While the video was being filmed, the abductor was back in the park. Can you imagine what he was doing in the park? He was following the youth group, keeping tabs on their progress toward the end of the laser tag course. Eventually, he used his cell phone to notify the filmmakers that the group was about ready to load the bus. That was their clue to stop the film, give the student his clothes back, and return him to the parking lot.

Before the filmmakers released him, they threatened to kill his parents if he dared to tell anyone what had happened. They also informed him that the man who had grabbed him had, during the day, made pictures with his cell phone camera, of the other teens in the group. If the student didn't cooperate, then those photos would be used in other pornography videos.

The student was completely frightened and worried. He told no one what had happened. Several months went by. His parents noticed that he had become more and more withdrawn, his grades were falling, and he never wanted to go out with friends. They tried to get him to open up. They did everything they could think of. Nothing seemed to help.

Notes: _____

_____

_____

_____

_____

_____

_____

_____

_____

_____

_____

_____

Notes: _____

_____

_____

_____

_____

_____

_____

_____

_____

_____

_____

_____

WHEN A CHURCH HAS MADE A serious commitment to a comprehensive plan for the prevention of abuse within its ministries, it will want to provide information about the plan to the congregation and parents.

Finally, the student went to see his pastor. He told the pastor that he needed to talk, but that he couldn't unless the pastor promised to keep the conversation confidential. The pastor agreed to listen, but instead of agreeing to keep his confidence, the pastor said, "No matter what the situation, I will help you get through it." The student told him everything, including the threats about killing his parents and using the photos of the other youth. When all of the story had been told, the pastor went home with the student to see his parents. Together, they called the police. In the end, the investigation not only corroborated the student's story; but, it also led the law enforcement authorities to a major operation of production and distribution of illegal pornographic material, including child pornography. Thanks to the courage of the student, the pastor, and the parents this criminal enterprise was brought to a halt.

This is a scary but true story that I wish had never happened. It illustrates so many of the dangers our youth face today, even when we, the adults, are doing all we know how to protect them. This incident shows how powerful and aggressive pornography predators are. It shows us how frightened our children and youth can be and the great lengths they will go to for the sake of protecting their families and friends. It also shows us that local law enforcement authorities can, and do, take these matters extremely seriously and they are prepared to protect us. Unfortunately, our law enforcement authorities don't often know where the dangers are until a child or teen victim comes forward.

I admit that everything about this story frightens me. It frightened me the first time I heard it and it still does because I know that children are still, on a daily basis, being abducted and abused for the profit of criminals. When I tell this story in a training session I can see the reactions on the faces of the participants. Until recently the most common reaction was a "Yes, but . . ." type of reaction. Someone would say, "Yes, but this must have happened in a big city—it couldn't happen in our town."

Here is what I learned when I began to research the facts about online predators and pornography. There are more than four million pornography websites in the United States. More than one hundred thousand of those provide illegal child pornography. There are more than two hundred forty-four million web pages in the United States alone; that is approximately 89% of the total number of pornographic web pages in the world. You can find this and more information at www.toptenreview.com and www.pewinternet.org. I have also found that in 2006 the revenue to the pornography industry in the United States was $13.3 billion dollars with $2.8 billion being generated from internet pornography. Worldwide, internet pornography revenue in 2006 was $4.9 billion dollars. Another significant fact is that in 2006, $2.19 billion in revenues was generated from the sale of pornography on cable television, pay per view channels, mobile devices, and phone sex sales. These figures make it clear that the technologies commonly and routinely used by our leaders in ministry to communicate with children, youth and families are very easily turned to dangerous purposes. We must be ever vigilant.

Here is another way to put the dangers in context for those who might want to say, "Yes, but . . .". Every second of every minute, 28,000 internet users are viewing pornography. Every second 372 internet users are typing adult search terms into search engines such as AOL, Yahoo!, and Google. Every second $3,075.64 is spent on pornography, and every thirty-nine minutes a new pornographic video is produced in the United States. Seeing information like this, from research projects such as the Pew Internet and American Life Project, makes it hard to continue to be a "Yes, but" type of parent, teacher, or minister. Information like this makes it easier to believe that one of every seven youth who are online receive sexual solicitations.

It is important to know that scary but true stories like I have shared are happening every day; but we cannot let such stories paralyze us and keep us from acting to create safety for our children and youth online. Here are some helpful guidelines for creating cyber safety for children, teens, parents, and all of us in ministry.

Safety tips for children:

1. Do not talk to people online that you do not know. You wouldn't talk to strangers in person, and you mustn't talk to strangers online.
2. Do not give out personal identification information such as name, address, phone number, name of your school, or a photo of yourself or your friends.
3. If you see something online that makes you uncomfortable, tell an adult. Don't try to solve the problem alone.
4. Stick to kid-friendly websites. Ask your parents to look at websites to make sure they are safe sites.
5. Avoid chat rooms at all costs. Avoid chat rooms at all costs. Avoid chat rooms no matter what.
6. Don't be a cyber-bully—don't say anything online that

Notes: _____

_____

_____

_____

_____

_____

_____

_____

_____

_____

_____

THE LIKELIHOOD OF ABUSE varies in different settings and circumstances. One aspect of planning for the safety of youth is arranging for appropriate settings.

Notes: _____

_____

_____

_____

_____

_____

_____

_____

_____

_____

_____

_____

Use e-mail to Communicate

only information related to youth ministry. The e-mail identity information of the group members should be protected and not be given out.

you wouldn't say in person, because once you say it online, you can never get it back.

7. Do not share your passwords with anyone except your parents. If you are using a public computer (such as in the public library), always be sure you delete your passwords before you leave to prevent anyone else from gaining access to your profiles, emails, or any other information.

8. Do not post anything online that you wouldn't want your parents or teachers to see.

9. Follow the rules your parents set for your computer use. The rules are to help keep you safe.

10. If you find that a friend has posted something online about you that is not safe (such as a photo or the name of your school), ask them to take it off. Tell an adult if your friend doesn't cooperate.

11. Never agree to meet in person with someone you have met online.

12. Always spend more time playing sports and talking with your parents that you spend online.

Safety Tips For Teens Using the Internet

1. Never post personal information on the internet that could you identify you to strangers. Do not post information such as your name, address, phone number, or the name of your school. Do not post photos of yourself and/or your friends wearing your school uniforms, standing in front of your school or home, or anywhere else that you could be found by someone who decided to try to look for you.

2. If you post any photos of yourself, your family members, or friends, alter the picture so that identifying information cannot be seen.

3. Do not post anything online about your friends or family members without their permission. Do not let your friends or family members post anything about you without your permission. Remember that anything posted on the internet is online forever and it can't be taken back.

4. If you must join a social networking website online, then create your profile with the maximum privacy settings available.

5. On your social network site profile page only accept online "friends" who are actually your friends in person.

6. Never agree to meet someone in person whom you have only met online.

7. Never respond to emails, instant messages, or text messages from strangers. You wouldn't talk to strangers in person and there is no reason to talk to strangers online.

8. Do not say, or post, anything online that you would be embarrassed for your parents, grandparents, coaches, or employers to see. Anything you post can be seen or found by anyone else, even if you think it is "private". Coaches, college admissions representatives and employers are making it a regular practice to check the internet to see what their team members, applicants or prospective employees have posted online.

9. Do not participate in cyber bullying on the internet, or with your cell phone. The messages you send can be traced back to you. If you are the victim of a cyber bully, tell an adult immediately.

10. Make sure to get your parents' approval before making any purchase or downloading any information/programs online.

11. If you receive messages that frighten you, or make you uncomfortable, do not ignore them. Go to an adult you trust for help.

12. Do not give out your password to anyone else except your parents.

13. Monitor and regulate the amount of time you spend online. Always spend more time with your family and friends face to face than you spend online.

14. Never give out your Social Security number online. Never give out a credit card number online without your parent's permission.

15. Stay out of online chat rooms no matter what. They are not safe.

16. Check your friend's profile pages often to be sure that they haven't posted things that might put you at risk.

17. Do not lie about your age to get into websites.

18. Show your parents your online profile pages from time to time. It is always good to let them know what you have posted.

Online Safety Tips For Parents

1. Learn what your children and youth know. Get educated about the powers and the dangers of the internet.

2. Teach your children to come to you any time they find something online that makes them nervous or uncomfortable.

3. Learn about privacy filters, anti-spyware, and firewalls so that you can use them to improve your family's safety online.

4. Keep your computer(s) in a family room, kitchen, or other area of the house where you and your kids are together.

5. Talk on a regular basis with your children and youth

Notes:
_____
_____
_____
_____
_____
_____
_____
_____
_____
_____
_____
_____
_____
_____

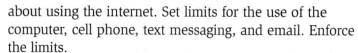

Notes: _____

_____

_____

_____

_____

_____

_____

_____

_____

_____

_____

_____

about using the internet. Set limits for the use of the computer, cell phone, text messaging, and email. Enforce the limits.

6. Be sure to review any photos your children want to post online. Don't allow them to post pictures that would give predators clues about where to find the children.

7. Look at the sites your children/youth see. If your teens have online profiles, look at them regularly with the teenager.

8. Ask your children/youth for their passwords. Tell them not to give their passwords out to anyone else.

9. Never allow your children and youth to have a personal meeting with someone they have "met" online.

10. Talk with other parents, and the youth ministry leaders, to find out what other families are doing to protect themselves online.

11. Take internet safety courses at your local high school or community college.

12. Collaborate with teachers, law enforcement officials, youth ministry leaders and other parents to provide greater knowledge for our children and youth and to assure a greater measure of safety for them.

Online Safety Tips for Ministers:

1. Do not post photos online of the youth group members. Use generic photos.

2. If you do post photos of the members, get parental permission to do so in advance.

3. Get advance parental permission to communicate with the youth group members by email, cell phone, instant messaging, or text messaging.

4. If you communicate by email, do not use "broadcast" emails. Use the "Bcc" option (blind carbon copy) so that each recipient sees only his or her address when a message is received.

5. Provide training classes for the youth to teach them how to use privacy settings for their social networking profiles and what things can be safely posted.

6. Encourage the children and youth to let you know if anyone they meet online tries to meet with them in person.

7. Develop policies regarding the use of cell phones, computers, and other technologies in ministry settings such as camping, retreats, and trips. Enforce the policies.

8. Teach the youth not to post, or say, anything online that they would not want you, or a coach, or an employer to see.

9. Collaborate with teachers, law enforcement officials, parents, and other community leaders to provide education-

al opportunities for parents and children/youth to learn how to be safe online.

10. Teach the children and youth to engage in face–to–face conversations with friends and family members more often than online conversations. By your own behavior, model respect for each individual member of the group.

There is far more to learn about cyber safety in ministry than we can include in this resource. Furthermore, everything we need to learn in order to be able to safely and effectively use technologies in our ministries is changing every day. In light of these facts, we must always be engaged in learning about the latest development, teaching parents, leaders, children and youth how to use communication technologies safely, and modeling the behaviors and values that we want our children and youth to adopt.

The Two-Adult Rule

Simply stated, the two-adult rule requires no fewer than two adults present at all times during any church-sponsored program, event, or ministry involving youth. Risk will be reduced even more if the two adults are not related. The Sunday school class is always attended by at least two adults. A Bible study group for youth is always taught by at least two adults. The youth fellowship group is always staffed with at least two adult counselors/leaders.

The significance of this rule cannot be overstated. A church will drastically reduce the possibility of an incident of abuse if this rule is followed. Abusers thrive on secrecy, isolation, and their ability to manipulate their victims. When abusers know they will never have a chance to be alone with potential victims, they quickly lose interest in working with youth. Thus, the youth are protected, and the church has greatly reduced the likelihood of a claim that abuse has been perpetrated by one of its volunteers or workers and reduced the likelihood of a claim of negligence against the church. Furthermore, vigilant adherence to the two-adult rule provides important protection to the church's workers with children and youth. Even small churches can adhere to this rule by using assigned adult roamers, volunteers who move in and out of classrooms and recreation areas and function as additional helpers. Parents and youth who know that two adults will be present at all times are less likely to make false allegations, since it would be nearly impossible to prove allegations against two workers. Church members will be more confident when they volunteer to work with youth, because they will know that they will never bear the total burden of

Notes: _____

_____

_____

_____

_____

_____

_____

_____

_____

_____

_____

_____

_____

_____

Notes:

_____

_____

_____

_____

_____

_____

_____

_____

_____

_____

_____

_____

leadership and that the church has made a commitment to protecting them as well as the youth.

First Aid/CPR Training

Providing first aid and CPR training on an annual basis for all church workers with youth is a basic step to assure the safety of youth. Of course, we all hope that first aid or CPR would never be needed in the church. Nevertheless, ministries with youth inevitably involve activities that can result in bumps, bruises, scrapes, or worse. Having workers who are prepared to deal with these competently goes a long way toward building the confidence of the youth and parents involved in the ministry of the church. In youth ministry, first aid competency is crucial on every trip, whether the group is going on a ski retreat or a mission project. Over the past four years, my church's senior-high youth group has gone on a ski trip each January. On each trip prior to this year, at least one youth skier was injured. The injuries ranged from bruises to concussions to broken bones. This year, one of the adult leaders broke his wrist. Adult leaders with good first aid training were a blessing on these trips.

Annual Orientation for Workers

All workers with youth—whether paid or volunteer, part-time or full-time, clergy or lay—should be required to attend an orientation session in which they are informed of the

- church's policies for the prevention of the abuse of youth;
- procedures to be used in all ministries with youth;
- appropriate steps to follow for reporting an incident of abuse of any of the youth;
- details of your state's laws regarding the definitions of child/youth abuse and the requirements of reporting abuse when it is discovered.

At this orientation the workers are given an opportunity to renew their covenant to abide by and cooperate with the church's policies and procedures. The church will have an updated record that it has informed all of its workers about its policies. Workers who do not attend should be contacted and asked to renew the covenant. The rate of turnover among workers with youth is high; therefore, you may find it prudent to offer this type of training every six months.

The Five-Years-Older Rule

Often, especially in youth ministry, the people who volunteer to work with or who apply for a paid position are in college or have just graduated from college. If a junior in college (age twenty or twenty-one) is recruited as a counselor in the senior-high youth fellowship, the counselor may be leading youth who are only three or four years younger than he or she is. This should be prohibited for the protection of the youth and of the worker. Nearly every church has members who can remember a situation in which this rule was not followed and the people involved came to regret it. Do not make the same mistake. College students might be successful as workers with the junior-high youth, or the middle-high group; but they should not be given the sole responsibility for any group.

No Workers Under the Age of Eighteen

When a church implements this rule, it goes a long way toward reducing the risks of injuries to its youth. A common practice in churches is to allow junior- and senior-high-aged volunteers in the church nursery. I have known of a church who used the junior-high youth to staff the infant nursery as a service project for the church. In effect, the church used children to supervise children. While in some situations they may provide excellent help, people under the age of eighteen cannot be expected to have developed the maturity and judgment that is needed to be fully responsible for younger children or younger youth. Putting children in charge of children invites disaster. Even in the context of using older youth to work with the younger group, you are taking unnecessary risks. Older youth sometimes abuse or bully their younger, smaller, and weaker peers. Many states have laws defining such behavior as child abuse and providing for significant sentences. It is not advisable or prudent to take the risk of relying on youth to lead themselves or their younger peers.

Windows in All Classroom Doors

Each room set aside for youth should have a door with a window in it or a half-door. A window in every door removes the opportunity for secrecy and isolation, conditions every abuser seeks. A half-door offers protection by offering full visual access to anyone walking by. Many pastors are adding a window in their study or office door to set a good example for the church and to protect themselves against false allegations of misconduct. Our youth need to be able to meet with one another and their adult leaders to study, worship, and fellowship in safety. Using areas that are visually accessible and classrooms that have windows in the door makes safe meetings possible by preventing would-be

Notes: _____

_____

_____

_____

_____

_____

_____

_____

_____

_____

_____

_____

_____

Notes: _____

_____

_____

_____

_____

_____

_____

_____

_____

_____

_____

_____

_____

_____

abusers from isolating an intended victim in a hidden or secret area.

Open-Door Counseling

At any counseling sessions with youth, the door of the room used should remain open for the entire session. Ideally, the session will be conducted at a time when others are nearby, even if they are not within listening distance. Counseling sessions conducted behind closed doors are a breeding ground for false allegations of abuse. Closed doors also make it too easy for the abuser to have the privacy and isolation he or she needs to carry out abusive acts. When one of our youth is troubled and seeks counseling, it is critical to resist the temptation to meet the youth in secret, even if the youth makes that request.

Limited Counseling Sessions

Whenever a youth seeks counseling, it is important to determine in the initial meeting if you are actually qualified to address the youth's needs effectively. If you do not believe you are sufficiently qualified, refer the youth to another counselor. In the event you do agree to counsel the youth, it may be prudent to agree to a limited number of sessions (two or three) and then refer the youth to another counselor if the problems have not been solved. In this way, if you cannot successfully help the youth, you will at least not unduly delay the counseling process with someone else.

Advance Notice to Parents

Providing parents with advance notice and full information about activities must be a guiding principle in a church's ministries with youth. Advance information encourages parents to support the ministry by scheduling their youth's participation. It could also possibly lead to parents participating in the ministry as volunteer leaders. Advance information can help parents and youth decide whether the content and substance of the event are suitable for their participation. Most importantly, advance information demonstrates that the church takes its ministries seriously enough to plan thoroughly and to provide for the safest possible experiences. For example, one Sunday evening the youth group activities at my church ended a little earlier than usual. When the other teens had already been picked up by their parents, my daughter was still there waiting for me. Even though our home is almost directly behind the church property and driving from the church to our home takes only a few minutes, the assistant youth director called me to ask if I would like for him to give her a ride or if I would prefer to pick her up. This was a good decision and a demonstration of good judgment from a risk-management perspective, but it was also good because he gave me full information and let me be involved in the choice. A parent who is informed, and even consulted, will surely be a parent supportive of the youth ministry.

Participation Covenant for All Participants and Leaders

A written covenant of participation should be developed and provided to all leaders and participants in youth ministries. The covenant is a statement in which the participants and leaders agree to

- take part in the ministry;
- give their best efforts to the ministry;
- respect the other participants;
- treat the others as well as they would wish to be treated.

Such covenants are useful (especially for retreats or trips) for establishing from the outset the behavior standards expected of everyone. The covenants are also important reminders for leaders that abusive behavior toward the youth will not be tolerated. This type of covenant can also be helpful in establishing a respectful code of conduct among the youth.

Parent and Family Education

When a church has made a serious commitment to a comprehensive plan for the prevention of abuse within its ministries, it will want to provide information about the plan to the congregation and parents. A family education event, or a series of events, in which families are invited to learn the facts about abuse and about the components of the church's plan is highly effective in disseminating full information to the maximum number of people in a minimum amount of time. An event of this type could include

- a speaker from your local law enforcement agency;
- a speaker from a local child protective services agency;
- a doctor or counselor who is experienced in treating abused youth;
- an attorney experienced in advising churches about risk management or loss prevention;
- a video about the incidence of sexual abuse of youth and children within churches;
- printed information about your state's abuse statutes and abuse reporting requirements;

Notes:

_____

_____

_____

_____

_____

_____

_____

_____

_____

_____

_____

_____

_____

89

Notes: _____

_____

_____

_____

_____

_____

_____

_____

_____

_____

_____

_____

- printed copies of your church's abuse prevention policies and procedures (allowing time for discussion).

Appropriate Equipment and Supervision

Ministries with youth are carried out in an endless variety of settings and locations: church sanctuaries, classrooms, camp cabins, athletic fields, retreat centers, tour buses, parks, and homes. Reports of abuse indicate that abuse happens in an equally large variety of settings. One aspect of planning for the safety of the youth participants is arranging for the ministry to take place in an appropriate setting. For instance, if the purpose of the ministry is weekly Bible study, then an appropriate setting would be a classroom at the church. If the purpose of the ministry is for the youth choir to travel for two weeks performing a musical in a dozen different cities, then the settings may include a tour bus, a series of hotel rooms, and a series of church sanctuaries.

The likelihood of the occurrence of abuse varies in different settings and circumstances. Bible study done in an open-doored classroom and in the presence of no fewer than two adults has a low probability of an incident happening. However, inadequate supervision of a youth choir at a hotel may increase the odds of an abuse incident. It is important for those planning ministries with children and youth to think through, in advance, the advantages and disadvantages of the settings they are considering.

Ministries with youth often involve using special equipment, and workers should know how to safely operate whatever equipment is needed. For instance, the youth group at my church has a Christmas tree sale each year to earn money for their summer mission trips. This project requires the use of handsaws, chainsaws (operated only by adults), hammers, ropes, and a calculator. Without adequate adult supervision and the ability of the workers to safely operate these items, the tree sale could turn into a disaster. Many youth groups participate in athletic events, such as rock climbing, rappelling, skateboarding, softball, basketball, and football. Activities like these need specific equipment, training, and supervision. When adequate training and supervision is not available, it would be better not to attempt the activity.

Other outdoor ministries would involve the need for specialized knowledge. Swimming or rafting events need a supervisor with lifeguard skills. When the ministry involves camping, hiking, and service projects such as Habitat for Humanity or the Appalachian Service Project, first aid and CPR skills are needed.

Adequate Insurance for the Scope of Your Ministries

Every local church needs to develop a good relationship with its insurance agent and to be adequately insured for the scope of its ministry. If the church is never involved in ministries in which people are transported in motor vehicles, then perhaps it can afford not to carry insurance for such occasions. However, for congregations involved with youth ministries, this is unlikely. Today, youth ministries need to be mobile more than ever before. Congregations, through their boards of trustees, should carefully consider all ministries and work with insurance agents to secure adequate coverage for them. Each local church that has adopted a plan for the prevention of abuse in youth ministry will be well ahead in the task of securing economical insurance coverage. If the church has not developed a plan for the prevention of such abuse, the insurance agent will be a valuable resource in supplying up-to-date information about the risks associated with abuse of youth in churches.

Transportation Options

It is often necessary in youth ministry to plan the best form of transportation for the project you are going to be involved in. The options often include cars, vans, and buses. Many churches have their own buses or vans that the youth group uses for trips. In such a situation, the adult leaders must be sure the vehicles are properly functioning, the church's insurance is up to date, and the adults who will be drivers are properly insured. Another possible alternative is to use commercial vehicles rented by the church and staffed with professional drivers. This option has advantages, especially if the trip is going to be a long one or you expect the traveling conditions to be hazardous. For example, you may be reasonably comfortable taking the senior highs on a weekend retreat in a couple of vans to a site only an hour or two from your church. On the other hand, if you are taking a group to a ski retreat that is five hundred miles away and the weather predictions are for snow and ice, using a commercial bus and professional driver would be a wise decision.

In the past couple of years, there have been some highly publicized accidents and wrecks involving youth groups traveling in fifteen-passenger vans. Studies have shown that these vehicles have a high propensity for rolling over. The National Highway Traffic Safety Administration has issued guidelines for operating fifteen-passenger vans more safely. The guidelines include not filling the van with more than ten passengers, not loading luggage or equipment on the top

Notes:

_____

_____

_____

_____

_____

_____

_____

_____

_____

_____

_____

_____

_____

_____

THE NATIONAL HIGHWAY Traffic Safety Administration has issued guidelines for operating fifteen-passenger vans more safely.

Notes: _____

_____

_____

_____

_____

_____

_____

_____

_____

_____

_____

_____

_____

of the van, and not overloading the cargo area at the rear of the van. If your church uses such a vehicle, exercise a reasonable amount of caution.

Special Settings

The procedures we've examined thus far have focused on local church settings. They are also applicable in other youth ministry settings. Settings outside the local church may include retreats, camps, mission trips, musical and drama productions, choir trips, lock-ins, service projects, and others. Anytime a trip is being planned, review your usual procedures to be sure you will be able to implement the appropriate ones on the trip.

Several facets of a trip, or a retreat, with the youth group need special attention. These include transportation plans, interpersonal boundaries in relationships, and sleeping arrangements.

Transportation plans: Be sure you have adequate and safe transportation for the trip. Address each of the following questions: Will we be able to have each passenger in a seat belt? Will we have enough space for the passengers to be reasonably comfortable and for all the luggage and equipment? Will we have a sufficient number of drivers who are qualified? Will we have first aid supplies? Will we have a cell phone or some other way to communicate in an emergency? Will we have a map and good directions?

Interpersonal boundaries in relationships: Trips provide wonderful opportunities for fellowship and nurturing positive and affirming relationships among the youth and adults in your group. You have more time to spend together and, thus, greater opportunities to interact. Just by doing normal things, such as cooking meals and cleaning up the kitchen or working on a mission project together, the youth have more chances for conversation—more sharing of their thoughts, opinions, hopes, and dreams—than in their usual settings. This interaction may be the greatest value of trips. It may also be the source of greatest risk. Before going on a trip, both the youth and the adult leaders must think through the needs for a simple and respectful code of conduct.

Beginning with the concept that both the youth and the leaders are expected to treat others as they would want to be treated, the leadership team can outline any other specific expectations. Modeling positive nurturing relationships might include no profane language, no practical jokes that would

be physically harmful, no permission for boys to enter the room where girls are sleeping or for girls to enter the room where boys are sleeping, and no permission for two youth or one adult and one youth to separate themselves from the group. Keeping the focus on developing stronger relationships among the whole group, rather than on developing new romances, will help keep the group attentive to one another and minimize opportunities for couples to pair up.

The adults will provide great leadership by modeling appropriate behaviors. For example, adults who stay involved with the youth and in the presence of the youth, instead of pairing off or going solo away from the group, are providing good models. Adults who express affection for members of the group by hugging them in the presence of others can model affirmation for the youth without creating the perception that the personal space and privacy of the individual group member is being violated. As the leaders think about appropriate standards of conduct, the key factors to consider are that everyone should be expected to be present with the group when activities are going on and that opportunities for two youth or one adult and one youth to isolate themselves away from the group should be minimized.

Youth camping programs provide opportunities for youth to build interpersonal skills. Nearly every annual conference supports such programs, which give a large number of youth a chance to get away from their daily routines and learn profound lessons about interdependence in the community of faith. However, these ministries can also present risks for abuse. Typically, our summer camping programs are staffed by college students and young adults, which is usually safe and effective. However, the schedule should specify where staff members should be (with their camper groups or in areas reserved for staff) during lights out and other activities. In addition, the staff members should be trained to model appropriate behavior in all situations. For example, staff members should know how to respond to a request from a camper for a private conversation. In such an event, the camp staffer can offer to listen to the camper in a location where they could be seen but not heard, thus eliminating a chance for isolation of a camper and secret behavior that could be abusive. During the course of a week at camp, the campers and staff members will be involved in a wide variety of activities, from doing ordinary daily activities to hiking, swimming, camping out, playing sports, and worshiping. Through all these events, the staff members must be attentive to carrying out the activities safely and to putting the best interests of the

Notes: _____

_____

_____

_____

_____

_____

_____

_____

_____

_____

_____

_____

93

Notes: _____

_____

_____

_____

_____

_____

_____

_____

_____

_____

_____

_____

campers first. If this is accomplished, the risk of abuse is diminished and the experience of camping will be happily remembered by the youth.

Sleeping arrangements: Today, safe sleeping plans are surely necessary when a youth group takes a trip. In days gone by, most trips were taken to church retreat centers, where all the girls slept in one large barracks-type room and all the boys slept in a similar room on the other side of the building. The female adult leaders slept in the room with the girls, and the male adult leaders slept in the room with the boys. The risks in these situations were most often a result of behavior among the members of the group.

In today's world, youth groups go on trips that require sleeping in public accommodations, such as hotels or dormitories on college campuses. Thus, the leaders must plan for minimizing the possibility of danger from within the group as well as from strangers. In addition, hotels typically provide sleeping rooms for two or four people. If four people are assigned to one hotel room, they will most likely have only two beds for the four to share. So, how can room assignments be made to maximize the safety of the youth and minimize the possibility of abuse? In a hotel-type setting, it is recommended that youth be assigned to rooms and adults be assigned to separate rooms. This would also be recommended for dormitory settings. If possible, make the room assignments so that an adult room is between two youth rooms. It is also recommended that the adults arrange among themselves to check on the youth rooms on a random schedule during the night. One youth group I know of is fortunate enough to have an adult leader who volunteers to take the night shift, staying awake and making sure there are no illicit comings and goings. Finally, if at all possible, choose a hotel where the rooms open to the interior of the building, rather than to the outside. This is crucial for minimizing the danger of strangers from the street.

It is obvious that these types of arrangements must be made carefully to protect the youth from abuse and to protect the adults from the possibility of false allegations. It may not be possible to eliminate every possibility of trouble, but prudent planning will help make things go as safely as can be reasonably expected.

Our Weekly Ministry Settings Are

1.

2.

3.

4.

5.

Our Summer Ministry Settings Are

1.

2.

3.

4.

5.

Our Ministry Settings Are Safe Because

1.

2.

3.

4.

5.

Notes: _____

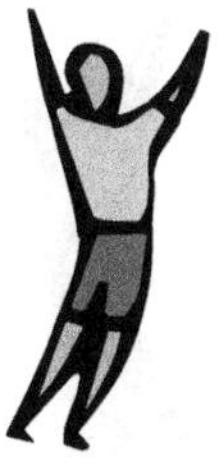

_____

_____

_____

_____

_____

_____

_____

_____

_____

_____

_____

_____

_____

_____

Notes: _____

_____

_____

_____

_____

_____

_____

_____

_____

_____

_____

_____

Our Church's Insurance Coverage Includes

1.

2.

3.

4.

5.

Our First Family Education Event Includes

1.

2.

3.

4.

5.

Part Four: Vulnerable Adults

Safe Sanctuaries for Senior and Vulnerable Adults

The Graying of the Church, by Richard H. Gentzler, Jr. was published by Discipleship Resources in 2004 and provides a wealth of information to guide us in the formation and implementation of ministries with senior and vulnerable adults. Since the first publication of *Safe Sanctuaries,* we have learned quite a lot about the correlation of those screening and operation procedures and ministries with senior and vulnerable adults. Furthermore, we have learned more about the prevalence of abuse of senior adults by those who have unsupervised access to them. Abuse of older adults comes in the same forms as child abuse: physical, sexual, emotional, ritual, and neglect. In addition, there is financial abuse of older adults within the context of ministries.

According to demographic information in *The Graying of the Church,* the older adult population in the United States is growing faster than the population of those under the age of eighteen. By 2010, 13% of Americans will be older than sixty-five and by 2030, more that 20% of Americans will be older than sixty-five. The seventy-eight million Baby Boomers will have reached retirement age. Twenty percent of our population is too large for the Church to ignore, or fail to engage in ministry! And yet, when we look at how congregations select and assign staff members for ministry, we find that for every one staff person assigned to work with older adults there are forty-seven staff persons assigned to work with youth. (See *The Graying of the Church,* p. 27)

A comprehensive, multi-dimensional approach to ministries with senior adults, as described in *The Graying of the Church,* will include opportunities for spiritual growth, enrichment learning, nutrition and fitness, intergenerational

Notes: _____

_____

_____

_____

_____

_____

_____

_____

_____

_____

_____

interaction, outreach, recreation, and service. As we plan these ministries, it is important and valuable to utilize Safe Sanctuaries screening and operating procedures.

Screening and Recruitment for Staffing Older/Vulnerable Adult Ministries

Include the same screening tools for reviewing applicants for Older Adult Ministries positions that your congregation uses for other positions. Our standards would include having a written application form, three personal references, a personal interview with the applicant, and a criminal background check of the applicant. It may not be necessary to use the "Five Years Older" rule when staffing your ministries with senior adults; however, using the "Six Month Hospitality Rule" for volunteers in these ministries is definitely helpful. The "Six Month Hospitality Rule" can be implemented for paid workers by making each offer of employment conditional upon the successful completion of a six month probationary period. Persons who are looking for new senior adult victims will not be enthusiastic about having no access to seniors for such a period of time.

The written application form will give us contact information as well as employment/volunteer history and reference contacts. A personal interview with each applicant gives the opportunity to observe the applicant and hear from him or her, first hand, about the experiences that are described on the application form. It will also provide an opportunity to evaluate the applicant's gifts and graces for ministry and ability to appropriately interact with older adults. Contacting the references provided by the applicant is certainly important. However, it is also useful to ask those references for additional persons who could be references. The time spent in this endeavor will be time well spent because, perhaps more than any other screening method, this will give a wealth of information about the applicant's relationships with older adults.

Finally, conducting a criminal background check of the applicant, for paid or volunteer positions, is needed. One type of abuse perpetrated against older adults, rather than children, is financial. Unscrupulous persons may seek out relationships with seniors and over time become so ingratiated with the seniors that they are given access to financial accounts and investments. In my law practice, I've seen a wide variety of attempts to take financial advantage of seniors. In many of these cases, conducting a criminal background would not have disclosed previous convictions for crimes such as embezzlement, theft, or fraud. However, conducting a criminal background check might well have discouraged the applicant by demonstrating that the church, or other placement entity (such as a home health care service or home repair business) was diligent in its efforts to seek only workers of the highest moral and ethical standards. Even when you think you know with certainty that the applicant has no criminal background, it is important to complete the background check and all the other parts of your screening process. Then, you can have confidence that you have diligently sought and found well-qualified persons for the positions you have to fill in ministries with older and vulnerable adults.

Training Volunteers and Employees for Ministries with Senior and Vulnerable Adults

Every state has elder abuse reporting statutes as well as child abuse reporting statutes. Our workers with senior adults need to be provided with the information necessary to make reports of elder abuse before the need arises; therefore, it is prudent to include this in our initial orientation and training.

First Aid and CPR training is important for those working with senior adults. Volunteers and staffers will need to know how to provide first aid for minor incidents. They will also need to know the new CPR recommendations and procedures. Many congregations have installed defibrillators on the premises for use in the event of certain cardiac emergencies. If your congregation has such equipment, then it is wise to train the staff members in the proper use of such equipment.

Training the volunteers and staffers in appropriate interpersonal boundaries and interactions with senior adults is vital. Maintaining appropriate interpersonal relationships will allow for development of strong friendships and fellowship within the context of our ministries and reduce the likelihood of those friendships being taken advantage of.

Older adults can provide a wealth of talent for volunteer ministry and they may have more time to give than middle-aged adults. The possibilities for older adults working within children and youth ministries seem endless, even in my limited imagination! One example that has worked out beautifully in my congregation is that of having older adults act as "Friends in Faith"—mentors to each of the youth in our

Notes:

Notes:

_____

_____

_____

_____

_____

_____

_____

_____

_____

_____

_____

_____

_____

Confirmation Class. Training for the older adults regarding appropriate interpersonal boundaries and interactions with youth is just as important to the success of such a ministry as training volunteers to work with the older adults.

Overall, training volunteers and staffers who work with older adults must include teaching the skills that are needed to carry out the full spectrum of your congregation's ministries. If your ministries include spiritual nurture, enrichment learning, nutrition and fitness programs, intergenerational events, outreach, and service opportunities, you will need to provide the training needed to successfully carry out each of these. Some training can be done in an annual orientation type of event and some of it may be best provided on a more frequent basis, for example, each quarter when the leadership changes in an enrichment learning program.

Operating Procedures in Safe Sanctuaries for Older Adults

Congregations planning for ministries with older adults must evaluate their facilities. If we are planning an event, will it be physically accessible for the participants? Will we need large print resources, assisted-hearing devices, or handicapped vehicles? The answers will, of course, be determined by the exact program or event being planned.

Generally, the following procedures will be helpful. Have two adults in every ministry setting as leaders. The importance of this for older adult ministries is the same as the importance for children's ministries and youth ministries. An abuser will have far less opportunity to abuse an older adult if he or she is not afforded the opportunity to lead without a partner and/or assistant. This holds true in every setting, whether the ministry is carried out at the church or in another location, such as Meals on Wheels or visiting in nursing homes or the homes of parishioners.

Carry out the ministries, such as Sunday School or Bible Study, in rooms where the door remains open, or there is an unobstructed window in the door. This helps to prevent the possibility of isolating an older adult behind closed doors where no one can see what is happing.

Counseling older adults can be successfully be conducted, maintaining confidentiality but prohibiting secrecy, by locating the counseling session in an office, or classroom where the door can be closed, but the window in the door can remain uncovered.

Traveling, for recreation and education, is often a part of ministries with older adults. The Prymetimers at my church seem to be on the go a lot! Trips to the mountains, to the beach, to see a museum or special garden, or to hear a concert are frequently on the schedule. Careful planning for transportation, accommodations, and meals will help assure the success of such trips. You will need to know the physical abilities of the participants. For example, will you have anyone who needs assistance with a wheelchair? Will you have anyone with special nutrition needs? Whatever your destination may be, advance planning and anticipation of exceptional circumstances will make the trip go more smoothly.

Other Groups of Vulnerable Adults

Your congregation may be in ministry with other groups of vulnerable adults, not just older adults. You may have ministries with developmentally disabled adults. You may have ministries with persons in hospice care. You may have ministries with prison inmates, probated offenders, or those who are homeless. The possibilities for ministry with such groups are perhaps limited only by our imagination. Conducting all of these ministries with Safe Sanctuary operating and screening procedures will give us the strong foundation we need to be able to continue to make disciples of Jesus Christ for the transformation of the world in every generation and every age group.

You will find excellent resources for planning ministry with older and vulnerable adults at **www.gbod.org**; **www.discipleshipresources.org**; and **www.aarp.org**.

Notes:

Part Five: Sample Forms & Resources

Developing a Congregational Plan for Responding to Allegations of Abuse

THE CONGREGATION'S PLAN for responding to suspected or alleged incidents of abuse of children, youth, or a vulnerable adult must be developed long before it may be needed. Two key components must be included in the plan: First, review your state's law for requirements in reporting suspected or known incidents of abuse to the department of family services or to the local police. Second, develop a plan for complying with the legal reporting requirements and for making statements to other officials, the congregation, and the media.

State Reporting Requirements

All workers must know their state's requirements in reporting abuse to law enforcement authorities and the department of family services. Each state has specific requirements, and you should consult a local attorney about what requirements are applicable to the workers in your church.

In some states, all workers with youth—either paid or volunteer—are mandated to report suspected cases of youth and child abuse when they have reasonable cause to believe that abuse has occurred or is occurring. The same requirements may apply to those who work with vulnerable adults. However, this is not true in every state. It is imperative to know what your state requires. In some states, ordained ministers are not mandatory reporters, even if they are appointed to work as ministers to children and families or as youth ministers. Instead, they are considered permissive reporters, which means they are encouraged to report when they have reasonable cause to believe that abuse

Notes:

_____

_____

_____

_____

_____

_____

_____

_____

_____

_____

Know Your State's
definition of elder abuse.

has occurred. Many state legislatures are reviewing their child abuse and other abuse reporting statutes and proposing modifications that will add clergy to the list of other specified mandatory reporters. Thus, as your congregation plans this year, it is important to get information on the most up-to-date statutory provisions.

Some states allow reports to be made anonymously, while others do not. If your state allows anonymous reports, it is advisable to take the precaution of making the report by telephone in the presence of an objective witness, such as the church pastor or the church's attorney, who can verify that the report was made (and by whom) in case this is needed later. Many states provide immunity for those making reports of elder abuse and child abuse in good faith. This means that the accused cannot bring a lawsuit against the reporter as long as the person had reasonable cause to believe that abuse had occurred.

Every state has statutory definitions of elder abuse, child abuse, and child sexual abuse. Workers must know these definitions to recognize whether or not the behavior they believe may be abusive meets the statutory definition. A local attorney, or the church's insurance agent, should be consulted to get the current definitions for your state.

Every state's elder abuse and child abuse statutes include a reporting time limit. Once a person becomes aware of or suspects abuse, he or she must report it to the proper authorities within a set amount of time. In some states, this is as short as twenty-four hours. Workers with youth may be subject to criminal penalties, by the requirements of state statutes, for failure to make appropriate and timely reports. Therefore, it is imperative that they be informed of these requirements. Workers must know the correct agencies to which they can report abuse. If state law requires that the local sheriff's department be contacted, the youth group counselor has not made a proper report by simply mentioning her suspicions of abuse to the youth coordinator.

Obviously, it is important to gather accurate information about your state's child abuse and elder abuse statutes before developing the church's reporting procedures. Contact the church's attorney, another local attorney, the local family services department agency, or your church's insurance company for help in gathering up-to-date information. Then draft a step-by-step plan for reporting any incident of actual or suspected abuse.

At this point, it will be necessary and important to educate and train all of the church's workers with youth, children, and vulnerable adults so that they are fully aware of their responsibilities under state law and under the church's prevention policies. Ideally, this education event will include the entire clergy and lay staff of the church; all full-time, part-time, paid, or volunteer workers; all parents of children and youth; and any others who are interested. Parents need to know that the people caring for their children and youth at the church are well informed and capable of taking appropriate actions in the event of suspected or alleged abuse. Clergy staff members, even if they are permissive reporters under state law, need to be informed of the law's requirements. **This cannot be overstated: Workers must be fully informed to be able to make lawful reports and to avoid possible criminal penalties for failure to report.**

Beyond the State's Requirements

The church's commitment to the prevention of abuse of elders, children, and youth requires that its workers make reports of abuse according to the requirements of state law. However, our obligations to respond to allegations go beyond the requirements of state law. As Christians, we must also be prepared to respond to others regarding allegations of abuse: the victim and his or her family, the news media, the church's insurance company, the annual conference, and possibly the abuser.

Faithful response to the victim will include taking the allegation seriously and respecting the victim's privacy, as well as providing sympathetic concern for the victim and his or her family. Faithful response to the victim does not condone blaming the victim or implying that the victim was in any way responsible for causing the abuse.

Faithful response to the annual conference will include notifying conference authorities (the church's district superintendent or the resident bishop) as soon as allegations of abuse are received. Conference authorities must be kept aware of the congregation's actions throughout the process, up to and including the final resolution of the situation. It will also be necessary to notify the church's insurance company if an allegation of child abuse is made.

Faithful response to the media can be one of the most frightening responsibilities for a local church. However, it can be accomplished fairly simply. In advance, designate one person who will speak to the media. This person may be the pastor,

Notes: _____

_____

_____

_____

_____

_____

_____

_____

_____

_____

_____

_____

_____

KNOW THE LEGAL REPORTING requirements for your state. Get up-to-date information from your church's attorney or insurance company.

Notes:

_____

_____

_____

_____

_____

_____

_____

_____

_____

_____

_____

_____

Know Your State's
definition of child abuse and child sexual abuse.

another staff member, the church's attorney, or a lay member of the church, such as the chairperson of the board of trustees. The person chosen must be capable of speaking calmly and thoughtfully in the glare of cameras and microphones. This person must be prepared to answer questions honestly without adding extra or unnecessary information. The designated spokesperson should be given permission to answer questions by saying, "I (we) don't know at this time." **None but the spokesperson should be authorized to speak to the media on behalf of the congregation.**

The designated spokesperson must be prepared to state the church's policy for the prevention of abuse, the church's concern for the safety of the victim and all youth and children, and the procedures the church has followed to reduce the risk of abuse to them. Speaking extemporaneously is tempting in situations such as this, but it is ill advised. The designated spokesperson will do well to have a prepared statement, or at least to have written notes so that the church's policies and procedures can be set forth clearly. The designated spokesperson should never make any statements indicating that the church does not take an allegation seriously or that the church suspects the victim has just made up the story to get attention. If the allegation involves the youth group, the designated spokesperson should not call on members of the youth group to answer questions or to make statements to the media.

Faithful response to the accused abuser will include acknowledgment not only that he or she is a person of sacred worth but also that he or she must stop the abusive behavior, prayerfully repent, and turn in a new direction. Faithful response will include removing the accused from his or her position as a worker with elders, youth, or children until the allegations are fully investigated and resolved. It does not necessarily mean that the accused will at some future time be placed again in a position of trust. Finally, faithful response does not include forgiving the accused before justice is achieved and the victim is ready to consider whether forgiveness is appropriate or not.

Not If It Happens But When It Happens
Since abuse of youth and children happens every ten seconds and in any location in the United States, it is not so unimaginable that a church could be called on to respond to an allegation of abuse. The local church that has made a commitment to the prevention of abuse in its ministry is

well on its way to being able to respond faithfully and effectively.

In summary, when an allegation of abuse of any of the children or youth is made against a worker or member, be prepared to do the following:

- Notify the parents of the victim and take any necessary steps to assure his or her safety until the parents arrive. **The safety of the victim must be the church's primary concern.**
- Do not confront the accused abuser with anger and hostility. Treat the accused with dignity, but immediately remove him or her from further involvement with the youth or children.
- Notify the proper law enforcement or department of family services agency.
- Notify the annual conference authorities, the church's insurance company, and the church's attorney.
- Keep a written record of the steps taken by the church in response to the allegations of abuse.
- Call on your designated spokesperson to make any necessary statements or responses to the news media.
- Prepare a brief and honest statement that can be made to the congregation without giving unnecessary details, placing blame, interfering with the victim's privacy, or violating any confidentiality concerns.
- Be prepared to cooperate fully with the investigation conducted by law enforcement officials or department of family services.

When a local church receives a report or allegation of abuse against a person who has been trusted with the care and nurture of its youth or children, it is immediately a crisis situation. The best and most faithful response is one that is planned in advance. By careful and thoughtful preparation, the congregation can provide a greater measure of love and concern for the victim and others involved while also cooperating, as necessary, with local authorities. Planning ahead will enable you to preserve your congregation's ability to surround the youth with steadfast love and establish him or her in faith strong enough to withstand any crisis.

What Do We Do Now?

I receive calls from church leaders on a regular basis. Each one tells me a similar story about a person who has approached the pastor, confessed to being a convicted sex offender, and now has asked to join the congregation as a

Notes: _____

_____

_____

_____

_____

_____

_____

_____

_____

_____

_____

_____

_____

_____

_____

WHAT DO WE DO NOW?

Notes: _____

_____

_____

_____

_____

_____

_____

_____

_____

_____

_____

_____

new member. Sometimes the offender has even asked to be a volunteer leader with children or youth! "What do we do now?" the leader asks me.

Over the past few years, a large number of convicted sex offenders have been released from prison and placed on probation. The legislatures of many states have enacted statutes that limit the locations where convicted sex offenders may be found for any purpose after being released from prison. Generally, these types of statutes do not make a church an acceptable location for the convicted offender, except, in some instances, for the single purpose of attending a regularly scheduled weekly worship service. Therefore, in order to respond appropriately to the convicted sex offender, the church leaders will need to get specific information from his or her probation/parole office regarding the restrictions that are placed on the terms of probation.

In 2004, the United Methodist Church at its General Conference adopted a resolution entitled "Church Participation by a Registered Child Sex Offender" (this resolution can be found in *The Book of Resolutions of the United Methodist Church*, 2004, as Resolution 355). The text of this resolution offers a reasonable plan of action a church can follow, after the church leaders have received specific information from the offender's probation/parole officer.

355. Church Participation by a Registered Child Sex Offender

The Social Principles of The United Methodist Church declare: "We recognize that family violence and abuse in all its forms—verbal, psychological, physical, sexual—is detrimental to the covenant of the human community. We encourage the Church to provide a safe environment, counsel, and support for the victim. While we deplore the actions of the abuser, we affirm that person to be in need of God's redeeming love."

Increasingly, churches are faced with a dilemma in their attempt to be faithful to both of the last two sentences above. Assuring the safety of children in our care, our facilities and our programs is a sacred duty. We must weigh that duty in the balance with what often seems the conflicting value of participation in the life of the church by a convicted child abuser. Being part of a worshiping community is not the only way for a person to experience God's redeeming love, but it is an important one.

Recent studies suggest a low likelihood that pedophiles can or will change. Without extensive professional treatment, virtually all child sexual offenders will re-offend. Repentance, prayer, and pastoral support, always in combination with lifelong professional treatment, can be crucial in helping to change behavior but, in themselves, offer slim hope of changing the behavior of perpetrators. Welcoming a child sex offender into a congregation must be accompanied by thorough knowledge, careful planning, and long-term monitoring.

A convicted and/or registered sex offender who wishes to be part of a church community should expect to have conditions placed on his or her participation. Indeed, offenders who have been in treatment and are truly committed to living a life free of further abuse will be the first to declare that, in order to accomplish that, they must structure a life that includes on-going treatment, accountability mechanisms, and lack of access to children.

The following steps should be taken in order to be faithful to the Social Principles' commitment both to safety from abuse and to ministry with abusers:

A. Local churches should:
- hold discussions in the church council and in adult education settings about the possibility of facing the situation of a convicted sex offender returning to or joining the church. These discussions should be held and general agreements reached about actions to be taken should the church find itself in this circumstance;
- develop a carefully constructed and openly negotiated covenant between the offender and the church community. The covenant should include agreements in the following areas: participation in a professional counseling program for at least the entire time of church membership or participation; adult "covenant partners" to accompany the offender while on church property or attending church activities; areas of church facilities that are "off limits;" restrictions on leadership in or on behalf of church; no role in church that includes contact with children or youth; any additional conditions for presence or participation; and
- assure that the covenant is maintained by having it written and signed by the offender, the pastor(s), and the chairperson of the church council. While confidentiality of victims should be respected, the

Notes: _____

_____

_____

_____

_____

_____

_____

_____

_____

_____

_____

_____

_____

Notes: _____

_____

_____

_____

_____

_____

_____

_____

_____

_____

_____

_____

_____

covenant should not be secret. Monitoring of the covenant should be taken seriously as a permanent responsibility.

B. Annual conferences should:

- develop similar plans and covenant for situations in which a convicted and/or registered sexual offender is involved or seeks involvement in the conference, its activities or facilities;
- include information about this concern and assistance with implementation of this resolution in its training and resourcing of clergy and local church lay leaders;

C. The General Board of Discipleship and the General Board of Global Ministries should:

- cooperatively develop and promote a process and specific guidelines to assist congregations in the education and covenant tasks outlined above.

ADOPTED 2004
Copyright © 2004, The United Methodist Publishing House, used by permission.

Following this action plan will allow the church and the convicted sex offender to develop a carefully constructed covenant between the church and the offender. The Participation Plan must be in writing and should include the specific restrictions of the offender's probation/parole, as well as all of the following:

1. The convicted offender's participation in a professional counseling program for the entire time of his/her participation and/or membership in the church.
2. There must be an adult "covenant partner" or covenant shepherd, who is present with the convicted offender at all times that he or she is on church property or attending any church activity that is off of church property
3. The action plan must clearly identify areas of the church property and facilities that are off limits to the convicted offender, including all areas used by children and youth and the restrooms.
4. The convicted offender's participation in worship, or leadership in any capacity in the church must be specifically detailed.
5. The convicted offender will be prohibited from having

any role whatsoever as a leader, volunteer, or member, that would involve contact with children or youth.

The entire Participation Plan must be put in writing and signed by the offender, the pastor(s), and the chairperson of the church council. In addition, it must be provided to the probation/parole officer of the convicted offender. Finally, there must be a clear and unambiguous provision that in the event the convicted offender fails to comply with any part of the plan, then his/her participation in the congregation will no longer be accepted and his/her probation officer will be notified.

When the church and a convicted sex offender agree to this Participation Plan, then it must be made clear through the church council that such an agreement must be monitored on a regular basis for the well-being of the children, youth, the congregation, and the offender. A convicted offender who truly has repented and seeks to lead a new life will want to have his/her participation witnessed and monitored because that is the only way to reduce the possibility of false allegations being made against him or her. By having a covenant shepherd with the offender at all times, the opportunity for false allegations to arise is reduced. Perhaps more important is the fact that by having a covenant shepherd with the convicted sex offender at all times, and in limited areas of the church property, the safety of the children and youth is less likely to be breached.

It will not be easy for any congregation to put this type of Participation Plan in place to accommodate a request from a convicted sex offender. Our congregations are dedicated to the safety of children and youth as they grow in faith. That dedication might make a congregation reluctant to try to include a convicted sex offender in worship, or in any other setting.

I often hear another question, "Why should we put such a thing as this together anyway? He has served his time and now he deserves some privacy." While it may be true that a convicted sex offender who has been released from prison has "served his time," it is not generally true, based on the statutes of many states, that he or she can keep his location and activities private. Every state has enacted statutes that require convicted sex offenders to register their residential information on a website that is available to everyone. Beyond the state mandated registries, there are many web-

Notes:

_____

_____

_____

_____

_____

_____

_____

_____

_____

_____

_____

_____

Notes: _____

_____

_____

_____

_____

_____

_____

_____

_____

_____

_____

_____

sites that also make such information readily available to the public.

There is one more important reason for engaging in a Participation Plan with a convicted sex offender if he or she requests such a plan. Every person, regardless of his or her criminal convictions, is a person of sacred worth. If we ignore the fact that a convicted child sex offender is participating with our congregation, then we may be failing to protect our children and we may also be failing to protect the convicted offender from new and false allegations of criminal behavior.

chapter nine

Implementation Strategies for the Congregation

FOR A CHILD abuse or elder abuse prevention policy to be successful, the entire congregation must wholeheartedly support its adoption and implementation. Universal support will not happen without a thorough and comprehensive plan for educating the congregation and for including a wide spectrum of members in the development of the policy and procedures.

The formation of a committee or task force, The Safe Sanctuaries Building Committee as it is often called, to prepare the policy and procedures should be a result of careful consideration. Whoever has responsibility for naming the membership of the task force (church council, council on ministries, administrative board) should invite representatives from any group that engages in ministry with children, youth, and vulnerable adults, Sunday school teachers, fellowship leaders, nursery workers, preschool workers, daycare workers, music ministry leaders. Parents and grandparents of children in preschool, elementary, middle-high, and senior-high grade levels should also be invited because they can make valuable contributions. By forming an inclusive task force you will reduce the likelihood of creating policies and procedures that will engender serious opposition from segments of the congregation. Instead, concerns can be brought to the task force and dealt with while the policy is still being developed.

As soon as the task force is named, it must meet and begin its work. Start by scheduling a series of at least six meetings. Set your meetings according to the projected completion date of the policy. Plan for each meeting to last approximately ninety minutes. There are several things that the task force will need to accomplish. These tasks include the following:

Notes: _____

_____

_____

_____

_____

_____

_____

_____

_____

_____

_____

_____

A COMPREHENSIVE PLAN HAS

- screening and training procedures for workers with children and youth
- reporting procedures for allegations of abuse
- a process for responding to allegations of abuse

- Research issues related to child abuse and elder abuse.
- Evaluate the current practices of your church related to the care and supervision of children, youth, and vulnerable adults.
- Develop new policies and procedures for the care and supervision of children, youth, and vulnerable adults.
- Develop a plan for responding to allegations of abuse.
- Develop a plan for responding to known incidents of child abuse and elder abuse.
- Present new policies and procedures to the church council or other approving body.
- Plan to educate the congregation about abuse and the new prevention policies.
- Plan training and periodic refresher training about the new policies for all church workers with children, youth, and vulnerable adults.
- Celebrate!

Task 1:
Research issues related to child abuse.

For the task force to effectively develop policies and procedures related to child abuse, it must have a solid foundation in basic information about abuse. Without this foundation the process of creating a prevention policy will be far more difficult, if not impossible. Some of this information could be provided to the task force in writing before the meeting, but plan substantial group discussion time. Steps in completing this task should include the following:

1. Review the definition and types of child abuse, using information from pages 29–30 and 61–62.
2. Review the statistics of the frequency of child abuse (pages 34 and 63–64).
3. Ask the members to think back over the past few weeks or months and recall incidents of child abuse that have made the news in the community. Ask the members to recall notices they have received about persons listed on the state Sex Offender Registry website who are residing in the church's area.
4. Have the members list the places and settings in which child abuse could occur in your congregation, such as: Sunday school, youth fellowship, youth choir, children's choir, other youth serving groups that meet in the church (Girl Scouts, Boy Scouts, and so forth), preschool/daycare, vacation Bible school, summer sports camps, and other ministries specific to your congregation.

5. Explore the question, "Who are the victims of child abuse?" Children and youth who are vulnerable as a result of being smaller, weaker, more isolated, or more trusting of adults are potential victims. (See pages 40–41 and 68–69 for more information.)

6. Explore the question, "Who are the abusers?" Abusers cannot be neatly stereotyped. Almost anyone can be an abuser under certain circumstances. There is no single personality type that is likely to become an abuser. There is currently no psychological test or tool that can accurately predict which person is, or will be, a child abuser. (See pp. 38–40 and 68 for more information.) It may be helpful for the task force to invite a resource person (such as the church's attorney or a representative of the local child protective services) to the meeting to present current information about abuse and abusers.

7. Explore the range of frequent reactions from abusers. These include denial, minimization, blame, anger, threats, and manipulation. Task force members, as well as congregation members, need to recognize the typical reactions. When child abuse happens and the abuser is confronted, any or all of these reactions may be displayed and may be very persuasive.

8. Review the consequences of child abuse in the church. The range of consequences include: psychological harm and/or injury to the victim; trauma and distress in the victim's family and the congregation; distress in the abuser's family; and possible legal damages and/or verdicts against the church.

Task 2:
Evaluate the current practices of your church related to the care and supervision of children and youth.

1. Explore the circumstances and situations in the church that could make it easier for an abuser to hurt a child. These could include inadequate recruiting and screening policies and practices for hiring workers with children and youth, inadequate supervision of workers, and inadequate control of workers and ministry settings, including a lack of observation and/or evaluation of the workers. Even if your church utilizes only volunteer workers with children and youth, there must be adequate supervision and evaluation to assure that ministry is being accomplished safely. When the task force members have identified the circumstances that make

Notes: _____

_____

_____

_____

_____

_____

_____

_____

_____

_____

_____

_____

_____

EVERY CONGREGATION IS capable of assuring that its church building is a place of security and peace for children!

Notes: _____

_____

_____

_____

_____

_____

_____

_____

_____

_____

_____

_____

_____

Faithful Response to the

victim will include

-taking the allegations seriously.

-respecting the victim's privacy.

-assuring the victim's safety.

abuse possible, they will be better able to understand and identify the ways that abuse can be prevented. Then the task force can move on to developing and integrating a comprehensive prevention policy.

2. Identify current policies. Even if there is no written policy, your church is undoubtedly operating under a set of unwritten rules that the members simply understand to be "the way things are done." For instance, if your church has no written policy regarding the supervision of youth on a summer mission trip, there is likely an understanding among the parents, youth, and workers about who can serve as chaperones for the trip and how many will be needed. The task force needs to identify the current practices of the church, whether written or unwritten, and begin to decide which are adequate, inadequate, and/or in need of modification.

3. Review the current policies regarding the recruitment and screening of workers with children, youth, and vulnerable adults, including paid workers, volunteers, and clergy staff members. Review the current policies related to training workers regarding child abuse and how to report allegations and/or incidents. Review the policies for supervising workers with children and youth. Review the current practices of how children and/or youth are disciplined to determine whether the methods used are appropriate and whether corporal punishment is excluded. Review the facilities used for ministries with children and youth to determine whether they are suitable. For instance, are the facilities too isolated from the rest of the church? These facilities should not be isolated but should provide openness and visibility for the participants—as well as for the parents coming to pick up their children.

Task 3:
Develop new policies and procedures for the care and supervision of children and youth.
At this point, the group will begin to integrate what it has learned about child abuse and the current circumstances in the congregation. As the new policies are developed, the following practical components need to be considered:
- recruitment and screening practices
- applications
- references
- disclosure forms
- background checks/consent forms
- covenant statements

- use of appropriate facilities for ministries with children and youth
- appropriate types of discipline for children and youth

The sample forms on pages 139–156 will be helpful as the task force develops recruiting and screening forms tailored to the specific circumstances of your congregation. Since the task force will probably not be an ongoing group, it is also important to identify which group in the church will be responsible for the periodic review and updating of the policies and procedures.

Task 4:
Develop a plan for responding to allegations of child abuse.

Even though the task force has drafted child abuse prevention policies and procedures related to the recruitment, screening, and selection of workers, it must include a plan for responding to allegations of abuse if they occur. The primary goal must always be to protect the victim. The task force will also need to plan for reporting allegations or incidents of elder abuse.

Furthermore, any plan designed for your congregation must comply with the laws of your state and local jurisdiction. This resource provides helpful ideas, but it cannot substitute for a consultation with your parish attorney or a local attorney familiar with the current requirements for reporting allegations of child abuse and elder abuse. It would be appropriate to present a written copy of the state laws about child abuse reporting requirements. It would also be helpful to invite a resource person to meet with the task force to interpret the state child abuse and elder abuse reporting statutes.

In addition, your response plan should designate a person (or several people) who will receive reports of abuse in the congregation and follow through on them, according to the requirements of your state law. This can be a clergy staff person, a Sunday school volunteer, or anyone else who is trusted. However, it must be someone who will honor the confidentiality of the reports. When a report or an allegation of abuse is received, these people must be prepared to follow the response plan. They need to remember that, generally, children do not lie about abuse. However, they also need to be aware that false allegations can be made, especially in circumstances involving custody battles. Knowledge about child abuse and familiarity with the

Notes:
_____
_____
_____
_____
_____
_____
_____
_____
_____
_____
_____
_____

FAITHFUL RESPONSE TO THE news media includes honest answers, even if that can only be, "We don't know."

Notes:

_____

_____

_____

_____

_____

_____

_____

_____

_____

_____

_____

_____

FAITHFUL RESPONSE TO THE annual conference includes notifying conference authorities as soon as allegations of abuse are received.

children and families of the congregation are important resources for the person receiving the report of abuse.

Your plan should also designate a person who will be responsible for any necessary communication with the media. This does not have to be the senior pastor. It can be any person who is capable of answering questions under pressure. Take care to designate only one person for this responsibility.

Be prepared to keep adequate documentation of any allegations of abuse. Keep incident report forms readily available. Sample forms can be found on page 150–151. **The information on the form must be kept confidential and limited to only those who must know,** such as the legal authorities specified by your state law, the pastor, the district superintendent, the bishop, the church's insurance company, the church's attorney, and possibly the chairperson of the staff-parish relations committee. Plan carefully who will have access to the forms and where they will be stored. It is advisable to keep records in a locked file. Emphasize the necessity of documenting all actions and conversations related to allegations.

Task 5:
Develop a plan for responding
to known incidents of child abuse and elder abuse.
These steps will be very similar to those for responding to allegations of child abuse. However, several additional components are necessary. Appropriate response to a known incident must include a plan for providing emergency care for the victim; a plan for notifying parents as well as legal authorities; a plan for protecting evidence; a plan for communicating with the media; a process for documenting every action taken and every report made; a plan for removing the abuser from any further contact with children; a plan for enlisting the full cooperation of the church staff; and a plan providing pastoral care to the victim and his or her family. Your congregation may also wish to include a plan for providing pastoral care for the family of the abuser. In some situations this may be more appropriately handled through a minister from a nearby church.

Task 6:
Present new policies and procedures
to the church council or other approving body.
When the task force has drafted the policies and procedures

outlined above, it will be ready to present its work to the church council or other approving body for endorsement and adoption. Ideally, the task force will have made regular progress reports and given the church council educational information regarding all of the issues related to child abuse and elder abuse prevention. Include in the presentation information about which group in the church will be responsible for periodic reviews of the policies and procedures.

Task 7:

Plan for educating the congregation about abuse and the new prevention policies.

This will be a shared responsibility of the task force and the church council. Educating the membership about abuse and the new policies cannot be accomplished in one meeting of the church council, or in one letter to parents, or in one article in the church newsletter. In developing these policies the members of the task force will come to understand how difficult it is to consider child sexual abuse, and elder abuse. Comprehension of the harm caused by the abuse does not come through one committee meeting. Similarly, full understanding as to how abuse can be prevented also takes time. The church council and the task force will be far more successful in reaching full support among the membership if they work together to inform the congregation, over time, about the pertinent issues and the plans being developed for prevention. Remember that people are more apt to respond to information that is presented in a variety of ways. Educate the membership through parent meetings, Sunday school classes, youth fellowship orientation and training meetings, newsletter articles, church bulletin inserts, video presentations, spoken words from the pulpit during worship, and letters from the task force.

Task 8:

Plan training and refresher courses about the new policies for all church workers with children, youth, and vulnerable adults.

An initial orientation and training of all workers with children, youth, and vulnerable adults should include information about the nature of abuse and its consequences, ways to prevent abuse, and ways to respond to abuse. The training should also educate the workers about the church's new abuse prevention policies and the plan for implementing the policies. A suggested training plan is provided in chapter 10. Finally, the task force and the church council

Notes: _____

_____

_____

_____

_____

_____

_____

_____

_____

_____

_____

_____

_____

_____

Faithful Response to the

accused abuser includes acknowledgment that he or she is a person of sacred worth in need of repentance.

Notes:

_____

_____

_____

_____

_____

_____

_____

_____

_____

_____

_____

_____

will need to designate a group in the church that will be responsible for providing ongoing training and orientation during the year for new workers with children and youth.

Task 9:
Plan for What To Do When An Abuser Wants To Join Your Church.

The task force may be the best equipped group in the congregation to lead a discussion on planning for this possibility. However, accomplishing this task should not be allowed to stand in the way of implementing the comprehensive Safe Sanctuaries policies and procedures for the protection of children and youth. In most cases, the church leaves this task until it is faced with a request from a convicted sex offender to join the congregation. Thinking through all the ramifications of such a request before it is made will provide the congregation, and the task force, with the opportunity to plan prudently and thoroughly without being pressured by time.

Task 10:
Celebrate!

A brief review of this chapter makes it plain that the implementation of a child sexual abuse prevention plan in your congregation will not be accomplished with one brief meeting and vote. The people who accept the invitation to serve on the task force developing the abuse prevention plan will be making a sizable commitment of time and energy. When their work is complete and your congregation has adopted a plan, there should be a great celebration!

Plan a time of commitment and rejoicing for the Sunday morning worship services and follow the worship with a celebration luncheon for the entire congregation. Use special music, banners, leaders, and plenty of children and youth to create the celebration. Give special recognition to the task force members, and express the congregation's gratitude for the work they have done. Focus the celebration on the congregational commitment to make your church a sacred and safe place in which all can encounter the love and saving grace of our Lord, Jesus Christ. A suggested order of worship is found on pages 157–158.

chapter ten

A Model for Training Workers

IMPLEMENTING A comprehensive strategy for the prevention of child abuse in a local church cannot be done without a substantial amount of education being provided for the workers with children and youth, the parents of children and youth, the congregation, and the children and youth themselves. This model is designed to be used with your church's workers with children and youth, but you may easily modify it for use with other groups. This model is designed to be used as a three- or a four-hour workshop. Providing this type of training will be an on-going necessity in each congregation. Whenever the volunteer leadership changes, for example at the beginning of the new Sunday School term in the fall, you will need to provide training for the new leaders. Whenever your state child abuse reporting statute changes you will need to provide training for the leaders. Many churches are utilizing training tools such as DVDs, power-point presentations, and their websites to make their training sessions more useful. Some helpful resources are listed in the final chapter of this book. Your congregation may choose to train your workers with vulnerable adults along with the children and youth workers. If so, be sure to include information on each age group in the training plans and materials.

I. Opening Worship

A. Prayer of Invocation

Gracious and most merciful God, you have brought us together in witness to your love of all children. Open our hearts and minds in this moment and prepare us to receive your message. Show us your will and fill us to overflowing with courage to face the reality of child abuse. Give us energy and dedication enough to make this, your church, a holy and hallowed place where all your children may be safe and secure as they grow in faith and in their knowledge of your presence in their lives! Amen.

Notes: _____

_____

_____

_____

_____

_____

_____

_____

_____

_____

_____

Education and Training

are essential for the successful implementation of policies and procedures to reduce the risk of abuse.

B. Suggested Scriptures

1. Exodus 22:21-23
2. Matthew 19:14
3. Luke 9:46-48

C. Brief Devotion

You may begin by recalling the baptismal ritual for children, reminding the participants of the pledge made by the congregation at each child's baptism. Acknowledge and list the many ways your congregation lives out that pledge through its current ministries with children. Conclude by introducing the child abuse prevention strategy as the newest component of your church's ministries with children and youth.

II. Introductory Information

A. Current Occurrences

Set the stage here for the substance of the event by introducing recent news reports from your own community's newspapers or television broadcasts related to incidents of child abuse in any locations and institutions. Also, in this section, you can present the news material related to any current litigation involving churches and claims of child abuse in your community.

B. Current Statistics

Quote the statistical information from this resource or from other sources available to you. Show the math problem from "Knowing the Facts" in chapter 3 on a power-point slide, chalkboard, or newsprint. It will also be helpful to show the other statistics found in "Knowing the Facts" for the whole group in the training.

C. Reasons to Implement a Child Abuse Prevention Strategy

1. Our church is a community of faith that can offer a safe haven and sanctuary where children and youth can seek advice, help, and nurture.

2. Our church is a place where more than just facts of child abuse can be taught. We can also teach and proclaim our Christian values: compassion, justice, repentance, and grace.

3. Our church is the place where children can come and learn and develop the inner strength and spiritual resources they will need to feel truly connected to God and to face suffering and evil.

4. Our church can be the place where children and adults are able to learn how to respond to painful and confusing events using the wisdom of the Scriptures.

D. Summarize

These reports and data demonstrate that we cannot ignore the possibility that abuse could happen here. For the sake of our children and the protection of our workers against false allegations, we need to intentionally work to prevent abuse.

III. What is Abuse and How Can We Recognize It?

Use the information on pages 29–30 to give definitions and indicators.

A. Physical abuse
B. Emotional abuse
C. Neglect
D. Sexual abuse
E. Ritual abuse

IV. Who Are Abusers? The Balance of Power

Use the information and examples provided on pages 38–40 and 68. Discuss the concepts of power and vulnerability and how these can lead to abuse. Use the news reports you shared earlier to help demonstrate the balance-of-power concept. In each account, have the participants list the sources of power available to the abuser. Then have the participants identify the factors that made the child vulnerable to the abuser.

If time allows, you may use a video here to illustrate the concepts you have just addressed. The bibliography and resource list at the end of this book provide suggestions of appropriate videos or sources for videos.

V. What Are We Doing to Keep Our Children and Workers Safe?

Present the new policies and procedures for the prevention of child abuse. Give participants time to read the policies. Allow time for questions and discussion as you review each section with the group.

A. Screening of Staff: Employees and Volunteers

Use your policies and the information in this resource for the substance of this section. Provide copies of all screening

Notes: _____

_____

_____

_____

_____

_____

_____

_____

_____

_____

_____

_____

_____

_____

HELP WORKERS WITH children understand that the policies are to protect the workers as well as the children.

Notes: _____

_____

_____

_____

_____

_____

_____

_____

_____

_____

_____

forms, application forms, covenant forms, consent forms, and position description forms. Allow time for a review of each form and for questions from the participants.

B. Training of Staff: Employees and Volunteers

Use your policies and the information in this resource for the substance of this section. Be thorough in reviewing all of the safety procedures, and allow time for questions.

C. Reporting Suspected Abuse

Use your policies and the information in this resource to explain the reporting procedure developed for your church. Explain the policy, the procedure for making a report, and the concept of confidentiality.

D. Completing the Task

If this is the first occasion the workers have had to see and review the screening, application, and position description forms, you may need to allow time for each of them to complete a form.

VI. Closing Worship

A. Covenant Forms

Have one or two people distribute covenant forms to the participants. Say, "We have reached the end of our time together today. Let's prepare to celebrate our church's commitment to protecting our children, youth, and those who work with them. Please read the covenant you have just received, and sign it as your commitment to our church's ministry with children and youth."

B. Return to the Scripture reading from the opening worship moments. Read aloud from Luke 2:21-24 and 2:40-52 or Luke 9:46-48.

C. Invite the participants to pray responsively with you by saying after each sentence prayer, "We welcome the children and youth!"

Leader: O God, by our presence here today,
People: *We welcome the children and youth!*

Leader: O God, by our promise in Holy Baptism,
People: *We welcome the children and youth!*

Leader: O God, by our participation in the ministries of this congregation,
People: *We welcome the children and youth!*

Leader: O God, by our commitment to keeping this place
  holy and safe in every way,
People: *We welcome the children and youth!*

Leader: O God, give us wisdom, strength, and courage
  enough to show the world that
People: *We welcome the children and youth!*

All: *Amen!*

D. Offering
  Ask the participants to bring forward their signed
  covenant forms as a sign of offering themselves in ministry with children and youth. Sing the Doxology.

E. Benediction
  May the grace of the Lord Jesus Christ, the love of God,
  and the power of the Holy Spirit guide and direct you in
  all you do. Amen.

Notes: _____
_____
_____
_____
_____
_____
_____
_____
_____
_____
_____
_____
_____

After Abuse, Then What?

chapter eleven

WHEN THE ABUSE of a child, youth, or vulnerable adult occurs in the church, there are many victims in addition to the one who has been physically harmed, and all are in need of healing ministry. Who are the other victims?

The other victims may include the

- family members of the child or vulnerable who was harmed.
- peers of the child or vulnerable adult.
- peers of the child's parents.
- remaining workers with children and youth and senior adults.
- congregation as a community of faith.
- family of the accused abuser.

Each victim will certainly need to be included in a ministry of comfort and healing.

Child abuse and elder abuse, either within the church or outside of the church, are not new phenomena. It has existed for longer than we can remember. What is a relatively new phenomenon is our recognition that the harm of abuse is exponentially magnified when it is kept secret within the church. Abuse that is hidden continues to cause anger, confusion, and fear in the congregation for years to come. I know of one congregation in which a youth was abused by an adult parishioner thirty-seven years ago, and to this day the real truth has not been shared with the whole congregation. As a result, the congregation has been paralyzed by feelings of anger and fear that have existed for so long now that many members cannot even verbalize the reason for the existence of these feelings. The congregation has a reputation among ministers for being an extremely depressing and difficult place to serve. In its local community, the congregation has a reputation of being an unfriendly and unwelcoming group of people. Clearly, failure to address the

Notes:

_____

_____

_____

_____

_____

_____

_____

_____

_____

_____

_____

Failure to Address the
issues of anger, fear, and grief that occur within the church after abuse can have far-reaching and devastating consequences.

issues of anger, fear, and grief that occur within the church after abuse can have far-reaching and devastating consequences for everyone.

How then can your church be in ministry to all, or any, of the victims of child abuse? The reality of ministry after abuse is that it must be aimed at assuring justice for all and healing for those who are suffering. Neither justice nor healing can be achieved in a short time. Just as your congregation has probably spent a year developing its child abuse prevention policy and implementation strategy, it may spend a year or more working toward healing and justice after abuse actually occurs. There is not a workshop to sponsor, or a video to watch, or a speech to make that can create the measure of understanding needed for healing and for justice to be achieved. Ministry with victims, both the individual and the congregation, is very similar to ministry with those in grief. By thinking in those terms, you can begin to grasp the length of time needed for the victim(s) and the congregation as a whole to be restored to a feeling of health and justice.

The First Step

The first step in ministry with victims of child abuse in a congregation must be truth telling. This means engaging in honest communication about what has happened. Truth telling does not mean engaging in gossip or speculation. Above all, truth telling does not mean blaming the child victim in any way!

How will you engage in honest communication? Follow the procedures you have already planned for reporting an incident of abuse to law enforcement authorities and denominational officials. By the time you have done that, it is very likely that rumors will have begun to spread among the members of the congregation. At this point, it is important to provide honest and forthright information. This may begin with a letter to the members that briefly explains the incident and the initial action taken by the church. Such a letter should not include the identification of the child victim nor that of the accused abuser. On the other hand, it should include a statement of the actions taken to assure the safety of all the children and to assure your congregation's continuing ability to provide ministry to children and youth. This letter should dispel rumors and innuendo and assure everyone that everything possible has been done to provide for the safety of the victim(s) and to enable the safe continuation of the church's ministry.

The Congregational Meeting

A congregational meeting can prove to be a powerful aspect of the ministry of truth telling. However, if thoughtful and prayerful preparation for such a meeting is not done, it can become an occasion of anger and confusion. Therefore, schedule a meeting for a specific time and place and make plans for it. Do not simply say at the time of announcements in the Sunday morning worship service, "As you may have heard, there has been an allegation of child abuse in our church, and now is just as good a time as any to discuss what happened." An impromptu invitation can be far more harmful than helpful. It may force members to participate in a discussion that they would very much prefer to avoid. It may shock members who have heard no previous reports or rumors. It may cause some members to suddenly remember previous trauma in their lives and evoke severe emotional reactions. Such an approach may also insult the family of the child victim by making it appear that child abuse in your church is nothing more than an item on the list of Sunday morning announcements. The consequences of such a cavalier approach, in subsequent litigation, could be harmful for the church.

Plan carefully for a congregational meeting. Give everyone advance notice so they may choose whether to attend or not. Select the leaders for the meeting very carefully. In most situations, it will be important for the pastor to be one of the leaders, unless the pastor is the accused abuser. If that is the case, then the pastor must not be one of the leaders of this meeting. Also, in these meetings, it is important to have lay leaders present as well as representatives from the annual conference (usually the district superintendent fills this role). The lay leader(s) will be able to provide information about the actions taken by the church thus far. The district superintendent may not need to do anything more than reinforce the support of the annual conference as the congregation deals with this crisis. Even so, this is a valuable contribution and should not be overlooked. Finally, I believe the leadership team for the congregational meeting should include a qualified counselor who is not necessarily a member of the congregation. Inevitably, this meeting will elicit strong feelings and emotions. By having a counselor present, it is possible to help immediately those who experience strong feelings, instead of putting off or minimizing the feelings. Virtually every congregation has members who are actually survivors of child abuse. It is certainly likely that these survivors will be present for such

Notes:

_____

_____

_____

_____

_____

_____

_____

_____

_____

_____

_____

_____

MINISTRY AFTER ABUSE

must be aimed at assuring justice for all and healing for those who are suffering.

Notes: _____

_____

_____

_____

_____

_____

_____

_____

_____

_____

_____

_____

It is Far Better to Admit not knowing the answer than to speculate about the incident or the outcome.

a congregational meeting. A counselor's presence and availability may be helpful for these persons as well as many others.

Quite a number of annual conferences have formed Response Teams for the purpose of assisting local congregations in responding to allegations or incidents of child abuse. If your annual conference has a Response Team then it will be very helpful to consult with the leader of the team as you plan a congregational meeting. The Response Team will typically be able to assist in carrying out the congregational meeting and in providing counselors who can be helpful. For more detailed information regarding Response Teams, you may contact The General Commission on the Status and Role of Women at: **www.gcsrw.org**.

Meeting Agenda

What should happen in a congregational meeting following an incident of child abuse? Include the following elements:

- fact sharing
- small group sharing time
- closing moments of reflection and worship

Open the fact sharing by giving an accurate description of what has happened and what actions have been taken, or will be taken. Answer questions as accurately as possible without jeopardizing any ongoing investigation by the church or local law enforcement agencies. Protect the identity of the victim(s), especially if the family has requested as much privacy as possible. Do not be afraid to answer questions with, "We don't know the answer to that yet." It is far better to admit not knowing the answer than to speculate about the incident or the outcome.

The small group sharing time probably will be the most important segment of this meeting. Divide the total group into small groups of five or six persons. Assign a prepared facilitator to each group. Your annual conference Response Team may be able to provide the facilitators for the meeting or suggest qualified persons from your local community. The facilitator will begin by letting everyone know that is is permissible to express *any* emotion within the small group. All will be allowed time to share, and there will be no debate about the feelings or emotions expressed. The purpose of this segment of the meeting is to help people identify and verbalize their feelings about the incident. The purpose is not to strategize a response or elicit premature forgiveness toward the abuser. Be prepared for this part of the meeting to take an hour or more.

When it is apparent that the small groups are able to bring their time together to a close, reassemble the whole group. Acknowledge the reality of this painful situation and offer a prayer for the congregation as it seeks to achieve justice for all involved and healing for all who are suffering.

Continuing Ministry

The initial actions of the church are really only the first steps in what may be a long process of restoring the victim(s) and the congregation to spiritual health. One letter or one congregational meeting probably will not be all your church needs. Based on the feelings, fears, and needs expressed in the congregational meeting, you can develop a plan for continuing ministry. It may be useful to appoint a task force for this planning process, just as you utilized a task force to develop the child abuse prevention policy and procedures. Another approach is to use existing groups within the church to plan appropriate ministries of healing, justice, education, and worship. Your annual conference Response Team, if you already have one, would most probably have members who are qualified to assist with planning for the ministries of healing, justice, education, and worship.

As the group begins its work, it will be well advised to consider several types of ministry: educational, supportive, and any others that have been suggested by members of the group.

Educational ministries may include programs on

- the consequences of child abuse.
- how to comfort families suffering from abuse.
- how children and youth can protect themselves from abuse.
- resources in your community for victims/survivors.
- other topics of concern.

Programs may include speakers who are adult survivors of child abuse, and they can tell how they achieved healing and recovery. Programs like these can be carried out through Sunday school classes, youth groups, or other settings. It is important to remember that none of these programs should be provided without advance notice and

Notes: _____

_____

_____

_____

_____

_____

_____

_____

_____

_____

_____

_____

_____

THE MORE A CONGREGATION
does to encourage openness and honesty in communication, the faster healing and recovery can proceed.

Notes: _____

_____

_____

_____

_____

_____

_____

_____

_____

_____

_____

_____

_____

publicity. In this way you ensure that those who wish to participate can make their plans and that those who do not wish to participate can avoid any involvement.

Support ministries can be developed within your congregation for families suffering as a result of child abuse, as well as for victims of child abuse. Identify qualified leaders within your congregation or community, and enlist their aid in organizing support groups. Providing individual counseling for the victim(s), the families, and other affected members of the congregation can also be a very important ministry. You may be able to make the necessary financial arrangements with a trained and experienced counselor so that the victim(s) and/or families can receive sufficient counseling to achieve healing. This type of ministry may also be important to the family members of the accused abuser. While it would be inappropriate to condone in any way the behavior of the abuser, it is appropriate to recognize that in this situation the extended family members of the abuser may suffer terribly. Offering counseling to them may be an act of grace and healing without condoning the abusive behavior.

Programming with children and youth aimed at restoring their trust in the church and in its workers will be a valuable support ministry. Programs and discussion groups that focus on justice, mercy, and reconciliation in difficult situations will set a solid foundation for their continuing spiritual growth. Programming of this nature will require extensive planning as well as qualified leadership. No matter how much work is required, it is worth it if one child or youth is enabled to feel safe in the church again.

All of these suggestions for continuing ministries are based on the premise that the more your congregation does to encourage openness and honesty in communication, the faster healing and recovery can proceed. No matter how long the process takes, there are two things that should never be allowed: blaming the victim and offering forgiveness to the abuser without any sign of repentance from the abuser. The child abuse victim is never responsible for being abused and did not do anything to cause it. Therefore, do not let your church attempt to assuage its conscience with words like, "Well, we did all we could to prevent something like this, but she asked for it!" This kind of remark does not foster open and honest communication.

Rather, it denies the truth and insults the victim and the victim's family.

There is no benefit to offering premature forgiveness to the abuser. For healing to occur, it is necessary that painful consequences be endured, not just by the victim(s) who suffers first but also by the abuser. Only when the abuser is truly able to live a changed life and demonstrate sorrow and repentance will it be possible for the congregation to offer the grace of forgiveness. Even then, the victim(s) may or may not be able to forgive the harm they have suffered, and no pressure to forgive should ever be brought to bear on the victim(s) simply to help the abuser feel better. Furthermore, we must be extremely cautious about allowing a convicted sex offender who is on probation/parole to become involved in the congregation. As has been previously discussed, such offenders may have specific and very strict restrictions as part of their probation requirements. It is not effective ministry to the victim(s), the abuser(s), or the other parishioners when we allow the convicted sex offender to become actively involved in the church without being fully aware of the legal restrictions that are included in the offender's probation and planning with those conditions in mind. Offering something called "forgiveness" to the convicted offender, without expecting full accountability from him or her, does not assist the offender in changing his or her behavior and it can be hurtful to the members who are victims or survivors of abuse.

Finally, after enough time has passed, the planning group may want to organize a time for sharing that is similar to that in the first congregational meeting. Use this to assess how much healing and recovery has occurred. Identify any remaining needs or issues that have not been resolved and possible ways to address them. There is a natural tendency to tuck the pain tightly away, creating the need for regular follow-up. In conclusion, provide a worship experience to express gratitude for the progress that has been made toward healing and recovery, and to express joy in the congregation's united efforts to do justice and to trust in the abiding grace and love of Jesus Christ, our Savior.

Notes: _____

_____

_____

_____

_____

_____

_____

_____

_____

_____

_____

_____

Sample Forms

PLEASE NOTE THAT all of the forms, checklists, and other items in this section are samples and need to be modified to meet your specific needs. Permission is given to reproduce these forms for churches who have purchased *Safe Sanctuaries*.

Items include

1. Membership Form for the Local Church Safe Sanctuaries Task Force

2. Child and Youth Abuse Prevention Policy

3. Employment Application

4. Authorization and Request for Criminal Records Check

5. Volunteer Application

6. Form for Reference Check

7. Participation Covenant Statement for Workers with Children and Youth

8. Report of Suspected Incident of Child or Youth Abuse

9. Accident Report Form

10. Local Church Self-Evaluation Form

11. Childcare Worker Position Description

12. Youth Ministry Staff Position Description

13. Director of Youth Ministry Position Description

14. Camper Cybersafety Form

15. Camp Employee Cybersafety Form

16. Order of Worship: A Safe Sanctuaries Celebration

MEMBERSHIP FORM FOR THE LOCAL CHURCH
SAFE SANCTUARIES TASK FORCE

Pastor
Name: _____
Address: _____
Phone: _____

Member of Staff-Parish Committee
Name: _____
Address: _____
Phone: _____

Member of Board of Trustees
Name: _____
Address: _____
Phone: _____

Lay Leader
Name: _____
Address: _____
Phone: _____

Minister of Youth/Director of Youth Ministries
Name: _____
Address: _____
Phone: _____

Minister of Children/Director of Children's Ministries
Name: _____
Address: _____
Phone: _____

Director of Any Weekday Program for Children
Name: _____
Address: _____
Phone: _____

Representative from Each Group Working with Children or Youth
(The number of members listed here will depend on the number of groups active in your congregation.)
Name: _____
Address: _____
Phone: _____

Name: _____
Address: _____
Phone: _____

Name: _____
Address: _____
Phone: _____

SAFE SANCTUARIES POLICY OF _____ CHURCH

Introduction

The General Conference of The United Methodist Church, in April 1996, adopted a resolution aimed at reducing the risk of child sexual abuse in the church. The adopted resolution includes the following statement:

> Jesus said, "Whoever welcomes [a] child...welcomes me" (Matthew 18:5). Children are our present and our future, our hope, our teachers, our inspiration. They are full participants in the life of the church and in the realm of God.
>
> Jesus also said, "If any of you put a stumbling block before one of these little ones...it would be better for you if a great millstone were fastened around your neck and you were drowned in the depth of the sea" (Matthew 18:6). Our Christian faith calls us to offer both hospitality and protection to the little ones, the children. The Social Principles of The United Methodist Church state that "children must be protected from economic, physical, emotional and sexual exploitation and abuse" (¶ 162C).
>
> Tragically, churches have not always been safe places for children. Child sexual abuse, exploitation, and ritual abuse ["ritual abuse" refers to abusive acts committed as part of ceremonies or rites; ritual abusers are often related to cults, or pretend to be] occur in churches, both large and small, urban and rural. The problem cuts across all economic, cultural, and racial lines. It is real, and it appears to be increasing. Most annual conferences can cite specific incidents of child sexual abuse and exploitation within churches. Virtually every congregation has among its members adult survivors of early sexual trauma.
>
> Such incidents are devastating to all who are involved: the child, the family, the local church and its leaders. Increasingly, churches are torn apart by the legal, emotional, and monetary consequences of litigation following allegations of abuse.
>
> God calls us to make our churches safe places, protecting children and other vulnerable persons from sexual and ritual abuse. God calls us to create communities of faith where children and adults grow safe and strong. (From *The Book of Resolutions of The United Methodist Church—2000*, pp. 180–181. Copyright © 2000 by The United Methodist Publishing House. Used by permission.)

Thus, in covenant with all United Methodist congregations, we adopt this policy for reducing the risk of abuse of children and youth in our church.

Purpose

Our congregation's purpose for establishing this Safe Sanctuaries policy and accompanying procedures is to demonstrate our strong and unwavering commitment to the physical safety and spiritual growth of all of our children and youth.

Statement of Covenant

Therefore, as a Christian community of faith and a United Methodist congregation, we pledge to engage in the ministry of the Gospel in ways that assure the safety and spiritual growth of all of our children and youth as well as all of the workers with children and youth. We will follow reasonable safety measures in the selection and recruitment of workers; we will implement prudent operational procedures in all programs and events; we will educate all of our workers with children and youth regarding the use of appropriate policies and methods; we will have a clearly defined procedure for reporting a suspected incident of abuse that conforms to the requirements of state law; and we will be prepared to respond to media inquiries if an incident occurs.

Conclusion

In all of our ministries with children and youth, this congregation is committed to demonstrating the love of Jesus Christ so that each child will be ". . .surrounded by steadfast love, . . .established in the faith, and confirmed and strengthened in the way that leads to life eternal." ("Baptismal Covenant II, *United Methodist Hymnal*, p. 44).

EMPLOYMENT APPLICATION

(This type of application should be completed by all who seek any position that will involve the supervision and/or custody of children or youth. You should tailor the application to the specific circumstances in your congregation. However, the employment application should include, at a minimum, sections for personal identification, job qualifications, experience and background, references, and a waiver/consent to a criminal records check.)

Name: _____
          Last   First   Middle

Are you over the age of 18? ☐ Yes   ☐ No

Present address: _____

City: _____ State: _____ Zip: _____

Home phone: _____

Position applied for: _____

Date you are available to start: _____

Qualifications:

Academic achievements: (Schools attended, degrees earned, dates of completion)

_____

_____

_____

Continuing education completed: (Courses taken, dates of completion)

_____

_____

_____

Professional organizations: (List any in which you have membership)

_____

_____

_____

First aid training? ☐ Yes   ☐ No   Date completed _____

CPR training? ☐ Yes   ☐ No   Date completed _____

Previous Work Experience: Please list your previous employers from the past five years. Include the job title, a description of position duties and responsibilities, the name of the company/employer, the address of company/employer, the name of your immediate supervisor, and the dates you were employed in each position.

_____

_____

_____

_____

_____

_____

Previous Volunteer Experience: Please list any relevant volunteer positions you have held and list the duties you performed in each position, the name of your supervisor, the address and phone number of the volunteer organization, and the dates of your volunteer service.

_____

_____

_____

_____

_____

_____

Have you ever been convicted of or pled guilty to a crime, either a misdemeanor or a felony (including but not limited to drug-related charges, child abuse, other crimes of violence, theft, or motor vehicle violations)? ☐ No ☐ Yes

If yes, please explain:

_____

_____

Employment Application, p. 2

References: Please list three individuals who are not related to you by blood or marriage as references. Please list people who have known you for at least three years.

1. Name:_____
   Address: _____
   Daytime Phone: _____
   Evening Phone:_____
   Length of time you have known reference: _____
   Relationship to reference: _____

2. Name:_____
   Address: _____
   Daytime Phone: _____
   Evening Phone:_____
   Length of time you have known reference: _____
   Relationship to reference: _____

3. Name:_____
   Address: _____
   Daytime Phone: _____
   Evening Phone:_____
   Length of time you have known reference: _____
   Relationship to reference: _____

Waiver and Consent:

I, _____, hereby certify that the information I have provided on this application for employment is true and correct. I authorize this church to verify the information I have provided on this application by contacting the references and employers I have listed, by conducting a criminal records check, or by other means, including contacting others whom I have not listed. I authorize the references and employers listed in this application to give you whatever information they may have regarding my character and fitness for the job for which I have applied. Furthermore, I waive any rights I may have to confidentiality.

In the event that my application is accepted and I become employed by _____ Church, I agree to abide by and be bound by the policies of _____ Church and to refrain from inappropriate conduct in the performance of my duties on behalf of _____ Church.

I have read this waiver and the entire application, and I am fully aware of its contents. I sign this consent freely and under no duress or coercion.

_____
Signature of Applicant   Date

_____
Witness   Date

This is a sample form. Please tailor your congregation's form to comply with the reporting requirements of the laws of your state and your congregation's policies.
Sample Employment Application, p. 3

AUTHORIZATION AND REQUEST FOR CRIMINAL RECORDS CHECK

I, _____ , hereby authorize _____ Church to request the _____ police/sheriff's department to release information regarding any record of charges or convictions contained in its files, or in any criminal file maintained on me, whether said file is a local, state, or national file, and including but not limited to accusations and convictions for crimes committed against minors, to the fullest extent permitted by state and federal law. I do release said police/sheriff's department from all liability that may result from any such disclosure made in response to this request.

_____

Signature of Applicant   Date

Print applicant's full name: _____

Print all other names that have been used by applicant (if any):

_____

Date of birth: _____ Place of birth: _____

Social Security number (if required by sheriff's dept.) _____

Driver's license number: _____ State issuing license: _____

License expiration date: _____

Request sent to: _____

Name: _____

Address: _____

Phone: _____

This is a sample form. Your congregation may prefer to conduct the criminal background checks on applicants through one of the many companies that now provide this service. The United Methodist Property and Casualty Trust (www.umcpact.org) can provide a website link to Trak-1 from which local congregations can obtain these services.

VOLUNTEER APPLICATION

Name: _____

Address: _____

Daytime phone: _____ Evening phone:_____

Occupation: _____

Employer: _____

Current job responsibilities and schedule: _____

_____

Previous work experience:_____

Previous volunteer experience: _____

_____

Special interests, hobbies, and skills:_____

How many hours per week are you available to volunteer? _____

_____ Days _____ Evenings _____ Weekends

Can you make a one-year commitment to this volunteer role?_____

Do you have your own transportation? _____

Do you have a valid driver's license? _____

Do you have liability insurance?(list policy limits and name of carrier) _____

Why would you like to volunteer as a worker with children and/or youth?

_____

_____

What qualities do you have that would help you work with children and/or youth?

_____

_____

How were you parented as a child? _____

_____

How do you discipline your own children? _____

Have you ever been charged, convicted of, or pled guilty to a crime, either a misdemeanor or a felony (including but not limited to drug-related charges, child abuse, other crimes of violence, theft, or motor vehicle violations)? ☐ No   ☐ Yes

If yes, please explain fully:

_____

_____

Have you ever been exposed to an incident of child abuse or neglect? ☐ No   ☐ Yes

If yes, how did you feel about the incident?_____

Would you be available for periodic volunteer training sessions? ☐ Yes   ☐ No

References: Please list three personal references (people who are not related to you by blood or marriage) and provide a complete address and phone information for each. References are confidential.

1. Name:_____

   Address: _____

   Daytime phone: _____

   Evening phone:_____

   Relationship to reference: _____

2. Name:_____

   Address: _____

   Daytime phone: _____

   Evening phone:_____

   Relationship to reference: _____

3. Name:_____

   Address: _____

   Daytime phone: _____

   Evening phone:_____

   Relationship to reference: _____

_____

                                  Signature of Applicant   Date

This is a sample form. Use it as a guide for tailoring your own application based on your congregation's needs.

Sample Volunteer Application, p. 2

FORM FOR REFERENCE CHECK

Applicant name: _____

Reference name: _____

Reference address: _____

Reference phone: _____

1. What is your relationship to the applicant?

2. How long have you known the applicant?

3. How well do you know the applicant?

4. How would you describe the applicant?

5. How would you describe the applicant's ability to relate to children and/or youth?

6. How would you describe the applicant's ability to relate to adults?

7. How would you describe the applicant's leadership abilities?

8. How would you feel about having the applicant as a volunteer worker with your child and/or youth?

9. Do you know of any characteristics that would negatively affect the applicant's ability to work with children and/or youth? If so, please describe.

10. Do you have any knowledge that the applicant has ever been convicted of a crime? If so, please describe.

11. Please list any other comments you would like to make:

12. Please list contact information for one additional person from whom we can obtain a reference for this applicant.

Reference inquiry completed by: _____

                                      Signature   Date

This is a sample form. Please tailor it to the specific needs of your local congregation.

SAFE SANCTUARIES PARTICIPATION COVENANT STATEMENT

The congregation of _____Church is committed to providing a safe and secure environment for all children, youth, workers, and volunteers who participate in ministries and activities sponsored by the church. The following policy statements reflect our congregation's commitment to preserving this church as a holy place of safety and protection for all who would enter and as a place in which all people can experience the love of God through relationships with others.

1. No adult who has been convicted of child abuse (either sexual abuse, physical abuse, neglect, emotional abuse, or ritual abuse) should volunteer to work with children or youth in any church-sponsored activity.

2. All adult volunteers involved with children or youth of our church must have been members of the congregation for at least six months before beginning a volunteer assignment.

3. Adult volunteers with children and youth shall observe the "Two Adult Rule" at all times so that no adult is left alone with children or youth on a routine basis.

4. Adult volunteers with children and youth shall attend regular training and educational events provided by the church to keep volunteers informed of church policies and state laws regarding child abuse.

5. Adult volunteers shall immediately report to their supervisor any behavior that seems abusive or inappropriate.

Please answer the following questions:

1. As a volunteer in this congregation, do you agree to observe and abide by all church policies regarding working in ministries with children and youth?   ☐ Yes   ☐ No

2. As a volunteer in this congregation, do you agree to observe the "Two Adult Rule" at all times? ☐ Yes   ☐ No

3. As a volunteer in this congregation, do you agree to abide by the "Six Month Rule" before beginning a volunteer assignment?   ☐ Yes   ☐ No

4. As a volunteer in this congregation, do you agree to participate in training and education events provided by the church related to your volunteer assignment?   ☐ Yes   ☐ No

5. As a volunteer in this congregation, do you agree to promptly report abusive or inappropriate behavior to your supervisor(s)?   ☐ Yes   ☐ No

6. As a volunteer in this congregation, do you agree to inform a minister of this church if you have ever been convicted of child abuse?   ☐ Yes   ☐ No

I have read this **SAFE SANCTUARIES PARTICIPATION COVENANT STATEMENT,** and I agree to observe and abide by the policies set forth above.

_____
Signature of Applicant   Date

_____
Print full name

This is a sample form. Please tailor it to fit your congregation's specific needs.

REPORT OF SUSPECTED INCIDENT OF CHILD ABUSE

1. Name of worker (paid or volunteer) observing or receiving disclosure of child abuse: _____

_____

2. Victim's name: _____

   Victim's age/date of birth: _____

3. Date/place of initial conversation with/report from victim: _____

_____

4. Victim's statement (give your detailed summary here): _____

_____

_____

_____

_____

5. Name of person accused of abuse: _____

   Relationship of accused to victim (paid staff, volunteer, family member, other): _____

_____

6. Reported to pastor: _____

   Date/time: _____

   Summary: _____

_____

_____

_____

7. Call to victim's parent/guardian: _____

   Date/time: _____

   Spoke with: _____

   Summary: _____

_____

_____

8. Call to local children and family service agency: _____

    Date/time: _____

    Spoke with: _____

    Summary: _____

    _____

    _____

9. Call to local law enforcement agency: _____

    Date/time: _____

    Spoke with: _____

    Summary: _____

    _____

    _____

10. Other contacts: _____

    Name:_____

    Date/time: _____

    Summary: _____

    _____

    _____

_____

Signature of Incident Reporter   Date

This is a sample form. Please tailor your congregation's form to comply with the reporting requirements of the laws of your state and your congregation's policies.

Report of Suspected Incident of Child Abuse, p. 2

ACCIDENT REPORT FORM

(Please print all information.)

Date of accident: _____ Time of accident: _____

Name of child/youth injured: _____ Age: _____

Address of child/youth: _____

_____

Location of accident: _____

Parent or guardian: _____

Name of person(s) who witnessed the accident: _____

   Name: _____ Phone: _____

   Name: _____ Phone: _____

   Name: _____ Phone: _____

Describe accident:

_____

_____

_____

_____

_____

Signature of Accident Reporter   Date

This is a sample form. Please tailor it to fit your congregation's specific needs.

LOCAL CHURCH SELF-EVALUATION FORM

Use the following list to help your congregation assess its policy needs for the prevention of child abuse in your church. Read each statement, and mark the appropriate response in the column to the right. By completing the form, you will be able to see at a glance the areas needing attention.

Statement	Yes	No	Unsure
1. We screen and check references for all paid employees, including clergy, who have contact with children or youth.	☐	☐	☐
2. We screen and check references for all volunteer workers for any position involving work with children or youth.	☐	☐	☐
3. We train at least annually all volunteer or paid workers with children or youth to understand the nature of child abuse.	☐	☐	☐
4. We train at least annually all volunteer or paid workers with children or youth in how to carry out our policies to prevent child abuse.	☐	☐	☐
5. Our workers are informed of state law requirements regarding child abuse and their responsibility for reporting incidents.	☐	☐	☐
6. We have a clear reporting procedure for a suspected incident of child abuse that follows the requirements of our state law.	☐	☐	☐
7. We have insurance coverage available in case a child abuse complaint occurs.	☐	☐	☐
8. We have a clearly defined building usage strategy as a component of our child abuse prevention plan.	☐	☐	☐
9. We have a clearly defined response plan to be implemented in the event an allegation of child abuse is made against someone in our church.	☐	☐	☐
10. We offer periodic educational opportunities to parents of children and youth about how to recognize and how to reduce risks of child abuse.	☐	☐	☐
11. We take our policies to prevent child abuse seriously, and we are committed to the enforcement of our policies for the safety and security of all our children and youth.	☐	☐	☐

CHILDCARE WORKER POSITION DESCRIPTION

Position: Childcare worker in the church nurseries
Reports to: Nursery Supervisor/Coordinator

General qualifications required

1. All childcare staff members shall be of good character and be of the Christian faith.
2. All childcare staff members shall
   a. be physically, mentally, and emotionally healthy.
   b. have a basic understanding of children and their needs.
   c. be adaptive to a variety of situations.
   d. be willing to grow in their knowledge of children through periodic education and training events.
3. All childcare staff members shall have a physician's report stating that the staff member is in good
   health and has presented the result of a current Tuberculin test.
4. _____ Church hires without regard to race, sex, or national origin.

Educational qualifications required

All childcare staff members shall have completed the equivalent of a high school diploma.

Duties of childcare staff member

1. Provide physical, emotional, and intellectual support and stimulation to each child in your care, as appropriate for the circumstances.
2. Provide appropriate guidance to each child in your care.
3. Develop a relationship of trust and continuity with the children in your care, which will enhance each child's development of positive self images.
4. Provide support and assistance to parents when they arrive with their child.

Performance expectations of a childcare staff member

1. Be punctual. Notify the nursery supervisor in advance if you must be late.
2. Be reliable in your attendance. Notify the nursery supervisor in advance if you must be absent.
3. Attend periodic training and education events provided by the church.
4. Be polite, friendly, and courteous to others, both children and adults.
5. Do not engage in physical punishment/discipline of any child.
6. Cooperate with other childcare staff and with parents.
7. Abide by and apply the childcare policies of _____ Church at all times.

I have read the position description for childcare staff members of _____
Church and understand its contents. My signature below indicates my agreement and covenant to abide by the requirements set forth above.

_____
Signature of Applicant   Date

This is a sample form. Please adapt it to the specific needs of your congregation.

CAMP _____ POLICY
ON SOCIAL NETWORKING AND BLOGGING

FOR VOLUNTEER LEADERS AND CAMPERS

In general, Camp _____ views social networking sites (e.g. MySpace), personal websites, and Weblogs positively and respects the right of campers and adult volunteer leaders to use them as a medium of self-expression. If a person chooses to identify himself or herself as a camper or volunteer leader at our camp on such Internet venues, some readers of such websites or blogs may view the camper or adult volunteer as a representative or spokesperson of the camp. In light of this possibility, our camp requires, as a condition of participation in the camp, that campers and adult volunteers observe the following guidelines when referring to the camp, its programs or activities, its campers, and/or employees and volunteers, in a blog or on a website.

1. Campers and volunteer leaders must be respectful in all communications and blogs related to or referencing the camp, its employees, other volunteers, and other campers.

2. Campers and volunteer leaders must not use obscenities, profanity, or vulgar language.

3. Campers and volunteer leaders must not use blogs or personal websites to disparage the camp, its employees, other volunteers, or other campers of the camp.

4. Campers and volunteer leaders must not use blogs or personal websites to harass, bully, or intimidate campers, volunteers, or employees of the camp. Behaviors that constitute harassment and bullying include, but are not limited to, comments that are derogatory with respect to race, religion, gender, sexual orientation, color, or disability; sexually suggestive, humiliating, or demeaning comments; and threats to stalk, haze, or physically injure another person.

5. Campers and volunteer leaders must not use blogs or personal websites to discuss engaging in conduct that is prohibited by camp policies, including, but not limited to, the use of alcohol and illegal drugs, sexual behavior, sexual harassment, and bullying.

Any camper or adult leader found to be in violation of any portion of this Social Networking and Blogging Policy will be subject to immediate disciplinary action, up to and including dismissal.

(This policy was adapted from the policy developed by Anne Horton for Camp Sumatanga)

CAMP _____ POLICY
ON SOCIAL NETWORKING AND BLOGGING

FOR EMPLOYEES

In general, Camp _____ views social networking sites (for example MySpace, Facebook, etc.), personal websites, and Weblogs positively and respects the right of employees to use them as a medium of self-expression. If an employee chooses to identify himself or herself as an employee of our camp on such Internet venues, some readers of such websites or blogs may view the employee as a representative or spokesperson of the camp. In light of that possibility, our camp requires, as a condition of employment at the camp, that each employee observe the following guidelines when referring to the camp, its programs or activities, its campers, its volunteer leaders, and/or other employees, in a blog or on a website:

1. Employees must be respectful in all communications and blogs related to or referencing the camp, its campers, and/or other employees and volunteers.

2. Employees must not use obscenities, profanity, or vulgar language.

3. Employees must not use blogs or personal websites to disparage the camp, campers, or other employees of the camp.

4. Employees must not use blogs or personal websites to harass, bully, or intimidate other employees or campers. Behaviors that constitute harassment or bullying include, but are not limited to, comments that are derogatory with respect to race, religion, gender, sexual orientation, color, or disability; sexually suggestive, humiliating, or demeaning comments; and threats to stalk, haze, or physically injure another employee or camper.

5. Employees must not use blogs or personal websites to discuss engaging in conduct that is prohibited by camp policies, including, but not limited to, the use of drugs and alcohol, sexual behavior, sexual harassment, and bullying.

6. Employees must not post pictures of campers or other employees on a website without obtaining written permission.

7. Our camp does not host or sponsor a social networking site. The use of our copyrighted camp name or logo is not allowed without written permission from the Executive Director.

Any employee found to be in violation of any portion of this Social Networking and Blogging Policy will be subject to immediate disciplinary action, up to and including termination of employment.

(This policy is revised and adapted from the policy of Camp Sumatanga, developed by Anne Horton.)

A SAFE SANCTUARIES CELEBRATION

Prelude
"Jesus' Hands Were Kind Hands " (United Methodist Hymnal, No.273) or
"Jesus Loves Me" (United Methodist Hymnal, No.191)

Call to Worship

Leader: O God, by our presence here today,
People: *We welcome the children!*
Leader: O God, by our promise in Holy Baptism,
People: *We welcome the children!*
Leader: O God, by our participation in the ministries of this congregation,
People: *We welcome the children!*
Leader: O God, by our commitment to keeping this place holy and safe in every way,
People: *We welcome the children!*
Leader: O God, in this time of worship, fill our hearts with joy as
People: *We welcome the children!*
Leader: O God, give us wisdom, strength, and courage enough to show the world that
ALL: *We welcome the children! AMEN!*

Hymn of Praise
"This Is the Day!" (*United Methodist Hymnal,* No. 657)
(Lead the congregation in singing this hymn as a round: first group–the children's choir; second group–all male voices; third group–all female voices.)

Congregational Prayer
Gracious and most merciful God, you have brought us together in witness to your love of all children and youth. Open our hearts and minds in this moment and prepare us to receive your message. Show us your will and fill us to overflowing with courage enough to preserve our church as a safe and holy place where our children and youth may grow in faith and in their knowledge of your presence in their lives! Amen.

Pastoral Concerns
Silent Prayer
Pastoral Prayer
The Lord's Prayer

Old Testament Lesson
Micah 6:6-8 (Have a junior-high female read this passage. Or both a junior-high female and male could read it together, in unison, as a powerful and different way to proclaim the Word.)

Congregational Singing or Children's Choir
"I'm Goin'a Sing When the Spirit Says Sing" (*United Methodist Hymnal,* No. 333)
"We Are the Church" (*United Methodist Hymnal,* No. 558)

Gospel Lesson
Matthew 19:13-15 or Luke 2:41-52. Have the Gospel Lesson read by a senior high male.

Response to the Gospel

"Heleluyan" (*United Methodist Hymnal,* No. 78)

Epistle Lesson

1 Corinthians 13:1-13 (Have a nursery worker or a grandparent from your congregation read this lesson.)

Affirmation of Faith

(*United Methodist Hymnal,* Nos. 883 or 887)

Recognition of Task Force Members

Invite all members of the Safe Sanctuaries Task Force that developed the child and youth abuse prevention policy to come forward in the Sanctuary. Describe the work they have done, and express gratitude and appreciation for their service. Present a guardian angel lapel pin or other appropriate item as a token of appreciation for their work on behalf of the children and youth.

Recognition of All Workers with Children and Youth

Invite all members who work with children and youth to stand. Express gratitude and appreciation for their time and devotion to our children and youth. Lead in a round of applause.

Passing of the Peace

Offertory Anthem (by the congregation or youth choir)
"Morning Has Broken" (*United Methodist Hymnal,* No. 145)
"God of the Sparrow
        God of the Whale" (*United Methodist Hymnal,* No. 122)

Doxology

(*United Methodist Hymnal,* No. 95)

Sermon

"We Are Our Children's Safe Sanctuary" (based on the Gospel and Epistle lessons)

Invitation to Christian Discipleship

Hymn of Dedication

"Jesus' Hands Were Kind Hands" (*United Methodist Hymnal,* No. 273)

Benediction

Response Hymn

"Pass It On" (*United Methodist Hymnal,* No. 572)

Other Sources and Resources

These organizations have helpful information and resource materials about child abuse. Materials from these organizations are available upon request.

Organizations

- **FaithTrust Institute**
  2400 North 45th Street, #10
  Seattle, WA 98103
  www.faithtrustinstitute.org
- **Childhelp USA**
  15757 N. 78th Street
  Scottsdale, AZ 85260
  www.childhelpusa.org
- **Children's Defense Fund**
  25 E Street NW
  Washington, DC 20001
  www.childrensdefense.org
- **Christian Ministry Resources**
  617 Greenbrook Pkwy.
  Matthews, NC 28104
  www.churchlawtoday.com
- **General Commission on the Status and Role of Women**
  77 W. Washington St. Suite 1009
  Chicago, IL 60602
  www.cosrow.org
- **National Center for Missing and Exploited Children**
  699 Prince Street
  Alexandria, VA 22314-3175
  www.missingkids.com
- **National Center for Prosecution of Child Abuse**
  99 Canal Center Plaza, Suite 510
  Alexandria, VA 22314
  www.ndaa-apri.org
- **National Children's Advocacy Center**
  200 Westside Square, Suite 700
  Huntsville, AL 35801
  www.nationalcac.org
- **National Clearinghouse on Child Abuse and Neglect Information**
  330 C Street, SW
  Washington, DC 20447
  www.nccanch.acf.hhs.gov
- **National Court-Appointed Special Advocate Association**
  100 West Harrison Street
  North Tower, Suite 500
  Seattle, WA 98119
  www.casanet.org
- **Nonprofit Risk Management Center**
  1130 Seventeenth Street, NW, Suite 210
  Washington, DC 20036
  www.nonprofitrisk.org
- **Office of Children's Ministries**
  General Board of Discipleship
  PO Box 340003
  Nashville, TN 37203-0003
  615-340-7143
  www.gbod.org/children
- **Office of Ministries With Women, Children, and Families**
  Community Ministries
  General Board of Global Ministries
  475 Riverside Dr., Room 1549
  New York, NY 10115
  gbgm-umc.org/mission_programs/cim
- **Parents Anonymous, Inc.**
  675 West Foothill Blvd., Suite 220
  Claremont, CA 91711-3475
  www.parentsanonymous.org
- **Prevent Child Abuse America**
  200 South Michigan Avenue, 17th Floor
  Chicago, IL 60604-2404
  www.preventchildabuse.org
- **Risk Management Department**
  General Council on Finance and Administration
  1200 Davis Street
  Evanston, IL 60201
  www.gcfa.org/RiskManagementPage.htm
- **Your state and/or county child and family protective services department.**

Sources

These resources will guide you to many other helpful resources related to child abuse.

- *Behavioral Covenants in Congregations: A Handbook for Honoring Differences*, by Gilbert R. Rendle (Alban Institute, 1999).
- *Is Nothing Sacred?: The Story of a Pastor, the Women He Sexually Abused, and the Congregation He Nearly Destroyed*, by Marie M. Fortune (United Church Press, 1999).
- *Keeping the Faith: Guidance for Christian Women Facing Abuse*, by Marie M. Fortune (HarperSanFrancisco, 1995).
- *Living the Sacred Trust: A Resource on Clergy Misconduct of a Sexual Nature for Cabinets and Boards of Ordained Ministry of the United Methodist Church* (General Board of Higher Education and Ministry, 1999). Phone: 800-672-1789.
- *Love Does No Harm: Sexual Ethics for the Rest of Us*, by Marie M. Fortune (The Continuum Publishing Group, 1995).
- *Mission Accomplished: A Practical Guide to Risk Management for Nonprofits* (Second Edition), by Peggy M. Jackson, Leslie T. White, and Melanie L. Herman (Nonprofit Risk Management Center, 1999).
- *Not If, But When* (Public Media Division of United Methodist Communications, 1999). Item #11-44-5. Phone: 888-346-3862.
- *Predators: Pedophiles, Rapists, and Other Sex Offenders* by Anna C. Salter, Ph.D., order from www.specializedtraining.com
- *Preventing Child Sexual Abuse: A Curriculum for Children Ages Five Through Eight*, by Kathryn Goering Reid (The Pilgrim Press, 1994).
- *Preventing Child Sexual Abuse: A Curriculum for Children Ages Nine Through Twelve*, by Kathryn Goering Reid and Marie M. Fortune (The Pilgrim Press, 1989).
- *Reaching for the Light: A Guide for Ritual Abuse Survivors and Their Therapists*, by Emilie P. Rose (The Pilgrim Press, 1996).
- *Safe and Secure: The Alban Guide to Protecting Your Congregation*, by Jeffrey W. Hanna (Alban Institute, 1999).
- *Sexual Abuse Prevention: A Course of Study for Teenagers* (Revised Edition), by Rebecca Voelkel-Haugen (The Pilgrim Press, 1996).
- *Staff Screening Tool Kit: Building a Strong Foundation Through Careful Screening*, by John C. Patterson (Nonprofit Risk Management Center, 1998).
- *Survivor Prayers: Talking With God About Childhood Sexual Abuse*, by Catherine J. Foote (Westminster John Knox Press, 1994).
- *Taking the High Road: A Guide to Effective and Legal Employment Practices for Nonprofits*, by Jennifer C. Hauge and Melanie L. Herman (Nonprofit Risk Management Center, 1999).
- *The Book of Discipline of The United Methodist Church—2004* (The United Methodist Publishing House, 2004).
- *The Buck Stops Here: Legal and Ethical Responsibilities for United Methodist Organizations*, by Mary Logan (Discipleship Resources, 2000).
- *The First Three Years: A Guide for Ministry With Infants, Toddlers, and Two-Year-Olds*, edited by Mary Alice Gran (Discipleship Resources, 2001).
- *The Hidden Shame of the Church: Sexual Abuse of Children and the Church*, by Ron O'Grady ("Risk Book Series") (World Council of Churches, 2001).
- *Violence in the Family: A Workshop Curriculum for Clergy and Other Helpers*, by Marie M. Fortune (The Pilgrim Press, 1991).
- *Welcome the Child: A Child Advocacy Guide for Churches*, by Shannon P. Daley (Friendship Press, 1994).

Videos

- *Ask Before You Hug: Sexual Harassment in the Church* (31 minutes). Helps clarify what constitutes sexual harassment. Produced by United Methodist Communications. Available from EcuFilm, 800-251-4091.
- *Bless Our Children: Preventing Sexual Abuse* (40 minutes). Story of one congregation's efforts to provide abuse prevention information for their children. Available from FaithTrust Institute, 206-634-1903.
- *Caring Shepherds* (18 minutes). Created to help congregational leaders identify potential problems and develop policies to reduce the occurrence of sexual abuse and misconduct. Available from the Risk Management Department of the General Council on Finance and Administration of The United Methodist Church, 847-425-6560.
- *Hear Their Cries: Religious Responses to Child Abuse* (48 minutes). Provides definitions related to abuse, signs for recognizing abuse, and examples of how to respond. Available from FaithTrust Institute, 206-634-1903.
- *Truth, Lies, and Sex Offenders* by Anna C. Salter, Ph.D., order from www.specializedtraining.com